KT-467-532

Left **Portico of Pompey, Vaison-la-Romaine** Right **Provençal meadow**

Left **Spice shop, Marseille** Right **St-Tropez**

As a guide to abbreviations in visitor information blocks: Adm = admission charge; DA = disabled access; D = dinner; L = lunch

3

PROVENCE'S TOP 10

PROVENCE'S TOP 10

🏛10 Provence Highlights

Provence's top sights span the region's rich and varied history, from Roman arenas, isolated abbeys, and the palace of the medieval popes, to the more recent opulence of the belle époque era and the glamorous resorts beloved of the 20th-century jet set. Sunsoaked beaches, pretty villages nestled among lavender fields and a mountainous hinterland have inspired generations of artists, and continue to enchant every visitor to the area.

1 Palais des Papes
The honey-coloured walls and towers of this medieval palace, the seat of 14th-century pontiffs, dominate the delightful town of Avignon *(see pp8–9)*.

2 Grand Canyon du Verdon
The Verdon river flows through deep limestone gorges into the turquoise Lac de Ste-Croix, creating one of Provence's most stunning natural landscapes *(see pp10–11)*.

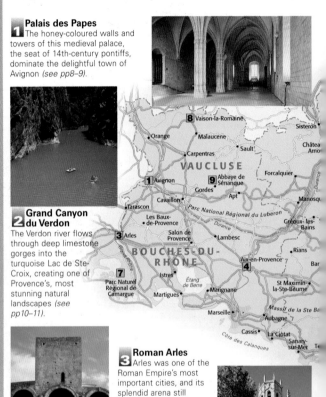

3 Roman Arles
Arles was one of the Roman Empire's most important cities, and its splendid arena still evokes the age of Caesar *(see pp12–13)*.

4 Aix-en-Provence
Cosmopolitan Aix is packed with fascinating museums and historic buildings. Nearby Mont Ste-Victoire inspired one of the greatest Provençal painters, Paul Cézanne *(see pp14–15)*.

7 The Camargue

Vast lagoons inhabited by wading flamingoes, and plains where native black bulls roam, are just part of the unique, protected landscape that is the Camargue (see pp20–21).

5 Vieux Nice

Nice is a lively and sophisticated city, but its Old Town retains a quieter, authentic character (see pp16–17).

8 Vaison-la-Romaine

A treasury of archaeological finds has been unearthed in this small town, once one of Provence's most important Roman sites (see pp22–3).

LPES-DE-
HAUTE-
ROVENCE

Seyne

St Etienne

Parc National du Mercantour

Colmars

Digne-les-Bains

Beuil

Forêt de Turini

St-André-les-Alpes

Entrevaux

Puget-Théniers

Sospel

Moustiers-
Ste-Marie

Castellane

ALPES-
MARITIMES

2 Grand Canyon du Verdon

Verdon

Vence

Menton

Monaco 10

ac de
te-Croix

Aups

Cagnes-sur-Mer

5 Cap Ferrat

Nice

Châteaudouble

Fayence

Grasse

Antibes

Juan-les-Pins

VAR

Draguignan

Cannes

Iles de
Lérins

Côte d'Azur

Miramar

Fréjus

St-Raphaël

Côte de l'Esterel

Ste-Maxime

Grimaud

6 St-Tropez

ssif des Maures

Collobrières

Le Lavandou

Hyères

20 ⌐————— miles ⌐0 ⌐ km ————⌐20

9 Abbaye de Sénanque

Set among beautiful lavender fields, the great Cistercian abbey is a wonderful example of Romanesque religious architecture (see pp24–5).

6 St-Tropez

Pretty and chic St-Tropez, with its yacht-filled harbour and gorgeous beaches, is the place to see and be seen on the Provençal coast (see pp18–19).

10 Casino de Monte Carlo

Walk in the footsteps of princes, courtesans and film stars at the Riviera's most dazzling example of 19th-century grandeur (see pp26–7).

Palais des Papes

In 1309, Pope Clement V transferred the papacy to France to escape political turmoil in Rome, and, for 68 years, Avignon became the religious, political and cultural centre of Christendom. The magnificent Papal Palace was built in just over 20 years, begun in 1335. Pope Benedict XII was responsible for the sober, Cistercian architecture of the Old Palace; his successor, Clement VI, added the New Palace in Gothic style, creating a massive ensemble of towers and stone walls soaring 50 m (165 ft) above the town centre. It remains a monument to the immense power of the papacy in the Middle Ages.

Consistory Hall

3 It was in the vast Salle du Consistoire *(above)* that the pope, cardinals and dignitaries gathered to consider key issues of the day. On the western wall now hang elegant 14th-century frescoes by Simone Martini.

Fresco, St John's Chapel

🕐 Arrive early – the palace receives up to 4,000 visitors a day in summer.

The palace's excellent hand-held audio-guides are available in seven languages.

Ask for the Passport when buying your first ticket to any Avignon sight – it entitles you to discounts of 20–50 per cent on entrance to other sites.

• Place du Palais, Avignon
• Map B3
• www.palais-des-papes.com
• Open Apr–Oct: 9am–7pm daily; Nov–Mar: 9:30am–5:45pm daily
• Adm €8.50 (audio-guide included); children under eight free

Top 10 Features

1. Courtyard of Honour
2. Treasury Halls
3. Consistory Hall
4. St John's Chapel
5. Refectory
6. St Martial's Chapel
7. Pope's Chamber
8. Stag Room
9. Great Chapel
10. Great Audience Hall

Courtyard of Honour

1 The "meeting" of the two palaces is the best place to compare the respective styles. While the Old Palace resembles a defensive keep, the New Palace has finer stonework. Today the courtyard *(below)* is the venue for theatrical events during the Avignon Festival *(see p58)*.

Treasury Halls

2 The papal wealth was stashed beneath the flag-stoned floor of the Lower Treasury Hall. The Upper Treasury Hall was effectively the accounts department.

St John's Chapel

4 Just off the Consistory Hall, this decorative gem *(above)* was created by Matteo Giovanetti, a leading Sienese artist. The now faded frescoes depict the lives of St John the Baptist and St John the Evangelist with exceptional use of perspective across the walls and arched vault.

5 Refectory

It was in the large refectory *(tinel)* that the pope entertained on feast days, eating alone on a dais, while cardinals and guests were arranged around the room according to rank. The vaulted wooden ceiling was restored during work carried out in the 1970s and the walls are now hung with 18th-century Gobelin tapestries.

7 Pope's Chamber

The pope's bedroom gives a sense of everyday palace life. The pontiffs slept within blue walls decorated with vine and oak-leaf motifs.

8 Stag Room

Clement VI let his extravagant tastes run wild in his study. Frescoes cover all four walls, with scenes of hunting and fishing against a forest background – the most unusual decor in the palace.

9 Great Chapel

Of massive proportions, 52 m (170 ft) long, 15 m (50 ft) wide and 20 m (65 ft) high, with seven vaulted bays, the Grande Chapelle *(above)* was the scene of all kinds of religious celebrations, including papal coronations.

10 Great Audience Hall

This was the meeting place of the Court of Apostolic causes, the popes' forbidding judiciary against which no appeal was allowed. The hall's vaulted ceiling *(left)* bears a small remaining section of the Prophet's Fresco – much of the fresco was hacked off and sold by soldiers during the palace's time as a barracks in the 19th century.

6 St Martial's Chapel

Livelier and more colourful than those in St John's Chapel, Giovanetti's frescoes here trace the life of a saint admired by Pope Clement VI. The works use deep blues, greys, browns and golds for an effect both realistic and miraculous.

Papal Avignon

The arrival of the papacy in Avignon brought great wealth and prestige to the town. When Pope Gregory XI took the papacy back to Rome in 1377 the French cardinals did not approve. On his death, they elected a French pope, while Italy elected an Italian one, putting the Christian world in schism. The row was resolved in 1417 and Avignon popes after Gregory XI have been considered anti-popes.

🔟 Grand Canyon du Verdon

The aptly-named Grand Canyon du Verdon is one of the most spectacular sights in France. Cutting deep into the rock, the Verdon river has created a series of gorges 25 km (15 miles) long and up to 700 m (2,300 ft) deep – a geography that prevented the area being fully explored until 1905. Vividly blue in places, foaming white where it storms through rapids beneath limestone cliffs, the Verdon flows south into the turquoise waters of the Lac de Ste-Croix, formed by damming the river close to Ste-Croix village. For the daring, the canyon offers rock climbing, whitewater rafting and hiking, while the 140-km (85-mile) drive around its magnificent landscapes takes a full day.

Notre-Dame-du-Roc, Castellane

🍴 Hotel-Restaurant la Provence (rte la Maline, La Palud sur Verdon, 04 92 77 38 72) is a good place to stop for lunch. Specialities include truffle omelette and rabbit *à la provençale.*

🚣 A whitewater, white-knuckle raft trip down the canyon is great fun and requires no rafting experience. Book in advance with one of the many operators in Castellane. The rafting and kayaking season is from April to September.

• Office du Tourisme, rue Bourgade, Moustiers-Ste-Marie, Map E3, 04 92 74 67 84, www.ville-moustiers-sainte-marie.fr, Open 11am–noon, 2–5pm daily
• Office du Tourisme, rue Nationale, Castellane, Map F3, 04 92 83 61 14, Open 9am–noon, 2–6pm Mon–Fri

Top 10 Sights

1. Route des Crêtes
2. Pointe Sublime
3. La Corniche Sublime
4. Martell Trail
5. Aiguines
6. Moustiers-Sainte-Marie
7. Lac de Ste-Croix
8. Trigance
9. La Palud sur Verdon
10. Castellane

①Route des Crêtes
The Route des Crêtes requires a good head for heights and close attention to the road, but rewards visitors with unbeatable vertiginous views across the most spectacular reaches of the canyon *(above).*

②Point Sublime
Close to the village of Rougon, Point Sublime *(right)* is one of the best places to look down into the rugged landscapes of the gorge. From here, the GR4 trail leads down into the canyon. Sturdy footwear is required, as is a torch (flashlight) to explore the tunnels cut into the cliffs.

③La Corniche Sublime
The drive along the Corniche Sublime (D71), on the south side of the canyon, lives up to its name. Stop at the Balcons de la Mescale for a superb view and marvel at Europe's highest bridge, the Pont de l'Artuby.

Martell Trail
4 Forming part of the much longer GR4 walking trail through the canyon, the Martell Trail is the most popular hike through the gorges, passing dizzying cliffs and crossing narrow passes *(see p57)*.

Aiguines
5 A stately 17th-century chateau, with tiled roofs and white turrets *(above)*, overlooks this attractive village. There are panoramic views over the lake.

Lac de Ste-Croix
7 The hydroelectric dam which created this 10-km (6-mile) long lake south of Moustiers in 1974 generates much of Provence's power supply. Electric motorboats, windsurfing boards and catamarans *(below)* can be hired at Ste-Croix village, on the west shore of the lake.

Trigance
8 This small, attractive village, with fine views of the rugged mountains which surround it, is a good place to stop for lunch on a motoring tour of the canyon.

La Palud sur Verdon
9 La Palud *(see p114)* is the base for organized walking expeditions into the canyon, whitewater rafting and kayaking on the rapids *(above)*.

Castellane
10 The pleasant, small town of Castellane is the largest community in the area and has the widest choice of places to stay and eat. Tour operators offer a range of activities in the canyon *(see p114)*.

Moustiers-Sainte-Marie
6 This lovely village *(right)* seems to grow out of the surrounding cliffs, with graceful stone bridges connecting houses on either side of the Ravine de Notre-Dame. Noted for its earthenware, it has a small museum and a 12th-century cliffside church, the Chapelle de Notre-Dame-de-Beauvoir *(see p112)*.

Roman Arles

One of the region's most charming old towns, Arles was originally founded by Greek traders but soon gained favour with Caesar and his successors and flourished into one of the most important provincial cities of the Roman Empire. Like many cities of the era, it was built to resemble a miniature version of Rome. Scattered around the narrow streets are relics of a lost empire, complete with the 4th-century remains of an emperor's palace, the remnants of a Roman circus and an arena where gladiatorial contests were staged, but all this gives only a hint of the town's wealth in Roman times.

Arles

Place du Forum is filled with outdoor cafés. Get there by midday to be sure of finding a table.

• Les Arènes, rondpoint des Arènes, Map B4, Open Mar–Sep: 9am–5:30pm, Oct–Feb: 10am–4:30pm daily, Adm €4.00
• Musée d'Archaeologique, presqu'île du Cirque Romain, Map B4, Open Mar–Oct: 9am–7pm, Nov–Feb 10am–5pm daily, Adm €4.00
• Thermes de Constantin, rue du Grand Prieuré, Map B4, Open Mar–Sep: 9–11:30am, 2–5:30pm, Oct–Feb: 10–11:30am, 2–4:30pm daily, Adm €4.00
• Les Alyscamps, ave des Alyscamps, Map B4, Open Mar–Sep: 9–11:30am, 2–5:30pm, Oct–Feb: 10–11:30am, 2–4:30pm daily, Adm €4.00
• Cryptoportiques du Forum, rue Balze, Map B4, Open Mar–Sep: 9–11:30am, 2–5:30pm, Oct–Feb: 10–11:30am, 2–4:30pm daily, Adm €4.00

Top 10 Sights

1. Les Arènes
2. Musée d'Archaeologique d'Arles
3. Théâtre Antique
4. Porte de la Redoute and Tour des Morgues
5. Thermes de Constantin
6. Les Alyscamps
7. Eglise St-Trophime
8. Egyptian Obelisk
9. Cryptoportiques du Forum
10. Place du Forum

1 Les Arènes
One of the most spectacular Roman relics in Provence, this well-preserved arena *(right)* has two floors of arches and seats for 20,000 spectators.

2 Musée d'Archaeologique d'Arles
The finest collection of Roman sculpture in Provence. Highlights include a marble statue of Emperor Augustus, a statue of Venus and a massive Altar of Apollo.

3 Théâtre Antique
All that remains of the Roman theatre are these two graceful columns *(right)*, nicknamed the "two widows". The theatre was once the hub of Roman Arles.

Les Arènes

4 Porte de la Redoute and Tour des Morgues
These battered gate towers stand either side of the former Via Aurelia, the highway which ran all the way from Arles to Rome.

5 Thermes de Constantin
A semi-circular apse marks the site of the once palatial bathhouse built in the 4th century, in the reign of Emperor Constantine.

For more Roman sights in Provence **See pp30–31**

7 Eglise St-Trophime

This spectacular Romanesque church, with its beautiful carved stonework *(left)*, was originally devoted to St Stephen. In the 10th century it became the church of St Trophimus *(see p32)*.

Roman Arles

RUE CONDORCER
RUE DE QUARE SEPTEMBRE
5
RUE DE LA CALADE
R. DU REFUGE
Arles
R. DES ARINES
1
PLACE DU FORUM
9 10
R. DE L'HOTEL DE VILLE
3 2
4
BOULEVARD EMILE COMBES
8 7
6

9 Cryptoportiques du Forum

This amazing labyrinth of chambers *(below)* beneath the ancient Forum was the city's granary, carved out of the ground during the 1st century AD.

10 Place du Forum

Nothing remains today but the name of the Forum, the market which was the very heart of Roman Arles. However the place du Forum is still the hub of the town.

8 Egyptian Obelisk

The square-sided obelisk with carved features *(below)* is likely to have been a trophy from Rome's conquest of Egypt during Emperor Augustus's reign.

6 Les Alyscamps

An avenue of marble sarcophagi *(above)* marks the site of the Roman necropolis where the city's dignitaries were buried. Among the many legends surrounding the site, it is claimed that Christ appeared here.

Arles Bullfights

Les Arènes was originally built to stage the gory gladiator contests so loved by the Romans, and today is still the scene of battles between man and beast. During the bullfighting season, every seat in the arena is filled. Most contests are Provençal-style, in which the bull is not killed, but Spanish-style *corridas* also take place.

🔟 Aix-en-Provence

Aix-en-Provence is a sophisticated town. Whether in the dignified squares and little streets of the Old Quarter or amid the town houses and tree-lined avenues of the 17th- and 18th-century district, the atmosphere is self-consciously graceful. But it's also lively and fresh: fountains are ubiquitous, as are students at one of France's oldest universities; the calendar of artistic events is rich; and the markets are the best in the region. The Romans called the town "Aquae Sextius", which evolved into "Aix", after the thermal springs which continue to flow here. From the 12th to 15th centuries, the town was capital of independent Provence and established itself as a cultural centre, a reputation further enhanced in the 19th century by local artist Paul Cézanne (see p36).

Façade, Musée Granet

🔲 The *calisson* is the traditional sweet of Aix, made with sugared almonds and crystallized fruit, and is available at *pâtisseries.*

• Office du Tourisme, 2 pl Général-de-Gaulle, 04 42 16 11 61, www.aixenprovence tourism.com
• Cathédrale St-Sauveur, pl de l'Université, Map C4, Open 10am–noon, 3–6pm daily, Free
• Musée Granet, pl St-Jean-de-Malte, Map C4, Open 10am–noon, 2–6pm Wed–Mon, Adm €3.00
• Atelier Cézanne, ave Paul Cézanne, Map C4, Open 10am–6:30pm daily, Adm €3.00
• Pavillon de Vendôme, 32 rue Celony, Map C4, Open 10am–noon, 2–6pm Wed–Mon, Adm €3.00
• Fondation Vasarely, 1 ave Marcel Pagnol, Map C4, Open 10am–1pm, 2–7pm daily, Adm €5.00

Top 10 Sights

1 Cours Mirabeau
2 Cathédrale St-Sauveur
3 Musée Granet
4 Atelier Cézanne
5 Rue Gaston-de-Saporta
6 Quartier Mazarin
7 Aix Market
8 Pavillon de Vendôme
9 Mont Sainte-Victoire
🔟 Fondation Vasarely

1 Cours Mirabeau
Created in 1650, Aix's majestic main avenue is a tunnel of greenery created by giant plane trees. In their shade stand elegant town houses and, on the northern side, smart, lively cafés. A succession of fountains adds freshness to the grandeur.

2 Cathédrale St-Sauveur
The focal point of medieval Aix *(right)*. Notable features are the octagonal, 5th-century baptistry, the 12th-century cloisters and a wonderful Buisson Ardent triptych painted in 1476 by Nicholas Froment.

3 Musée Granet
This lovely former priory is today home to a gallery of European art, dating from the 16th to 19th centuries.

4 Atelier Cézanne
Cézanne's studio from 1901 until his death has been left as it was – a jumble of artist's paraphernalia, furniture and still-life subjects *(left)*.

5 Rue Gaston-de-Saporta

Running from the town hall to the cathedral, is the liveliest thoroughfare of the Old Town, throbbing with commerce.

6 Quartier Mazarin

It was in this quiet district that the Aix nobility established some of their finest town houses in the 17th and 18th centuries. Within the tranquil sector of ornamental façades, small art galleries and charming antiques shops, the discreet, sober air of old money and aristocracy remains palpable.

7 Aix Market

The vast and colourful Aix market *(left)* colonizes all the town's old squares on Tuesday, Thursday and Saturday mornings. From the Place de Verdun via the Place des Prêcheurs to the Place de l'Hôtel de Ville, the streets come alive with stalls selling fresh produce, clothes and antiques.

8 Pavillon de Vendôme

Obliged to enter holy orders, local cardinal Louis de Mercoeur built this honey-stoned villa *(below)* as a love-nest for his mistress in 1665. Its size, decorated façade and extensive gardens, however, suggest a rather open secret. It now houses a collection of 18th-century paintings.

9 Mont Sainte-Victoire

To the east of Aix, this soaring mountain, 1,000 m (3,300 ft) high and 7 km (11 miles) across, exerts an almost mystical power over the region. Cézanne was so obsessed by its changing moods and intriguing shapes that he painted it more than 60 times. On the northern slopes is the Château de Vauvenargues, former home and burial place of artist Picasso *(see p36)*.

Aix-en-Provence

10 Fondation Vasarely

This intriguing centre *(above)* is dedicated to Hungarian artist Victor Vasarely's work on the integration of art into architecture. Behind the geometric façade are displays of weird dimensions and perspectives.

Exploring Aix

Start at the Office du Tourisme, opposite the Rotonde fountain on place Général-de-Gaulle. If you want to follow in Cézanne's footsteps pick up the walking tour leaflet here. Otherwise, stroll up Cours Mirabeau to No. 55 (Cézanne's childhood home, now La Plume En Or shop) and slip into the Old Town through the tiny Passage Agard. Return for a drink at the Café des Deux Garçons at No. 53 Cours Mirabeau, where Cézanne met other artists. Chic shops are in the Quartier Mazarin on the other side of the Cours.

Provence's Top 10

🔟 Vieux Nice

Numerous foreign aristocrats and sundry rich and famous may have colonized other parts of the city, but Old Nice, just below the castle hill, belongs firmly to the Niçois, who claim it with Mediterranean gusto. Tiny streets throb with arm-waving commerce; Baroque architecture slots in among hanging washing, galleries, craft workshops and food stalls. The noise, aromas and colour recall the city's long links with Italy – Nice became French as late as 1860. The atmosphere lasts well into the night in the many bars, restaurants and clubs.

Façade, Palais Lascaris

🍷 Resist free drinks on Cours Saleya; they're offered by restaurateurs trying to tempt you to a table.

🚗 Vieux Nice is for pedestrians only. There's parking on place Masséna, blvd Jean-Jaurès and Quai des Etats-Unis.

• Office du Tourisme, 5 prom des Anglais, Map H4, www.nicetourism.com
• Palais Lascaris, 15 rue Droite, Map H4, Open 10am–noon, 2–6pm Tue–Sun, Free
• Chapelle de la Miséricorde, Open Tue & Sun as part of Palais Lascaris tour only, Adm €3.00
• Cathédrale Ste-Réparate, pl Rossetti, Map H4, Open 10:30am–1pm, 2–6pm Tue–Sat, Free
• Musée de la Marine, pl 8 Mai 1945, Map H4, Open 10am–noon, 2–6pm Tue–Sun, Adm €3.00

Top 10 Sights

1. Cours Saleya
2. Palais Lascaris
3. Chapelle de la Miséricorde
4. Colline du Château
5. Cathédrale Ste-Réparate
6. Place St-François
7. Rue St-François-de-Paul
8. Quartier du Malonat
9. Rue Pairolière
10. Musée de la Marine, Tour Bellanda

Cours Saleya

1 The great square (or rather, oblong) bursts to life in the morning sun every Tuesday to Sunday with the world-famous flower market. Come evening, bar and restaurant terraces buzz. On Monday mornings the flower market is replaced by an antiques market. This is Old Nice's focal point, colourful and vigorous.

Palais Lascaris

2 From the façade to the grand staircase and 17th-century noble's apartments beyond, the scale and decor of this Baroque palace *(above)* is sumptuous.

Chapelle de la Miséricorde

3 If you see only one of Nice's Baroque churches, make sure it is this one. The splendour of the decoration makes it one of the world's best examples of the style.

Colline du Château

4 "Castle Hill" *(left)* was the stronghold of Nice until medieval times. The castle was destroyed in 1706, but the hill boasts breathtaking views.

5 Cathédrale Ste-Réparate

When the Dukes of Savoy ruled Nice they worshipped in this soaring, 17th-century church, beneath the majestic dome and within the extravagance of the stuccoed Baroque decor.

6 Place St-François

This delightful square *(left)*, overseen by an 18th-century clocktower and a Baroque palace, is the site of the daily fish and herb market, held around the dolphin fountain.

9 Rue Pairolière

Here, street commerce reaches its zenith. Food shops spill over with *socca* (pancakes), salt cod and spicy meats, jostling for space amid Provençal frocks and jewellery. It's a bracing turmoil of aromas, colours and Niçois accents.

10 Musée de la Marine, Tour Bellanda

French composer Hector Berlioz (1803–69) stayed here for a year in 1844. Now the tower, at the foot of the Colline du Château, houses an interesting maritime collection of weapons, model boats, instruments and paintings.

7 Rue St-François-de-Paul

This busy thoroughfare *(below)* is home to two Nice institutions: the Rococo Pâtisserie Auer at No. 7 and Alziari, olive and olive oil specialists, at No. 14.

8 Quartier du Malonat

Daily life courses through the tiny streets and squares, and beneath the washing and *trompe l'oeil* house decorations in the most authentic sector of Vieux Nice.

Baroque Churches

Vieux Nice is celebrated for its Baroque churches. In addition to those mentioned here, there are half a dozen others worth visiting: Ste Rita (rue de la Poissonnerie); Gésu (rue Droite); St Martin-St-Augustin (pl St-Augustin); St François-de-Paule (rue St-François-de-Paule), St-Suaire (rue St-Suaire) and the Chapelle des Pénitents Rouges (Rue Jules Gilly – Latin Mass every Sunday morning).

St-Tropez

Within the space of a short stroll it is easy to see why this sun-soaked, congenial fishing village, with its pretty harbour, red-tiled houses and fabulous sandy beaches, captured the heart of a generation of painters, Bohemians and later of holiday-makers. Despite all its hype as a world-famous tourism mecca of the rich and famous, "St-Trop" retains a good deal of its original charm – brightly painted fishing boats still moor in the Port de Pêche, although today they are increasingly outnumbered by gleaming yachts.

Eglise de St-Tropez tower

🍷 Le Café on place des Lices, formerly the Café des Arts, is where St-Trop's Bohemians hung out in the 1950s and 1960s heyday.

✪ Visit the place des Lices on Tuesday or Saturday morning, when the square is crammed with gorgeous flower, fruit and antiques stalls.

• Map F5
• Office du Tourisme: quai Jean Jaurès, 04 94 97 45 21, Open 9am–1pm, 2–7pm Mon–Sat
• Eglise de St-Tropez: rue de l'Eglise, Open 9:30am–noon, 2–4pm daily, Free

Top 10 Sights

1 Place des Lices
2 Citadel
3 Vieux Port
4 Musée de l'Annonciade
5 Plages de Tahiti and Pampelonne
6 Eglise de St-Tropez
7 Tour Suffren
8 La Ponche
9 La Fontanette
10 Sentier des Douaniers

Place des Lices
This market square *(below)*, immortalized by the painter Charles Camoins *(see p35)*, still has some of the atmosphere captured in his work. Crowded with open-air cafés shaded by plane trees, it is the perfect place to watch locals playing *pétanque (see p78)*.

Citadel
The 17th-century ramparts surround a fort built to protect the village from Barbary corsairs. There are fine views of the village from the walls.

Vieux Port
The quayside of the Old Port, quai Jean Jaurès *(above)*, is lined with leisure vessels year-round. In summer the waterside buzzes with artists, and pedestrians hoping for a glimpse of someone famous.

Musée de l'Annonciade
Close to the Vieux Port, a pretty 16th-century chapel has been wonderfully converted to house a world-class collection of paintings by artists connected with St-Tropez, including Bonnard, Derain, Dufy, Matisse, Rouault and Signac *(see p34)*.

5 Plages de Tahiti and Pampelonne

St-Tropez's beaches begin 4 km (2.5 miles) south-east of the town, on the long bay called the Anse de Pampelonne *(see p42)*. The 9-km (5-mile) sweep of sand is divided into smaller stretches, each with its own name.

7 Tour Suffren

Built in AD 880 by Guillaume I, Duke of Provence, this round tower overlooking the harbour was once part of a larger castle, the Château Suffren. Nearby, quai Suffren is the mooring point for flotillas of showy motorboats.

8 La Ponche

La Ponche *(left)* is the core of the original fishing village. With narrow streets, painted shutters and white-washed walls, it looks much as it did before tourism came along.

Artistic Mecca

How did St-Tropez transform itself from undiscovered fishing village to holiday hotspot? Painter Paul Signac *(see p37)* must take half the blame: he arrived on his yacht in 1887, fell in love with the place and decided to stay. Other painters followed, along with writers and would-be artistic types, attracted by warm weather and easy living. The film industry discovered the St-Trop scene in the 1950s, Brigitte Bardot became its ultimate symbol in the Swinging Sixties and the place has never looked back.

9 La Fontanette

The small La Fontanette beach, just east of La Ponche, is not as spectacular as those further afield, but is the only one within walking distance of town and ideal for a midday swim while exploring St-Tropez.

6 Eglise de St-Tropez

The ebullient, Italian Baroque church, built in the early 19th century, contains a gilded bust *(right)* of the town's patron saint, Tropez (or Torpès). The Roman legionary converted to Christianity and was martyred by Emperor Nero, but he was pushed out to sea by the Romans and his body was washed up where the town now stands.

10 Sentier des Douaniers

The "Customs Officers' Path" is part of a *sentier littoral* (coastal path) with spectacular views of the coast. The tiny pebbly or sandy bays *(above)* offer bathing opportunities away from the crowds. The energetic can follow the path for 35 km (21 miles) to Cavalaire.

🔟 The Camargue

Black bulls, white horses and pink flamingoes: these are the classic images of the Camargue delta where the Rhône meets the sea and Europe's only cowboys gallop across the flattest land in France. It's a 200,000-acre zone of lagoons, salt-flats and marshes; remote, romantic and rich in birdlife. Large stretches are protected and inaccessible, but open to all are the long evenings of gypsy music and wine as the sun sets on the horizon.

Camargue cowboy

🕙 For the real Camargue experience visit a *manade* (farm) open to the public.

Mosquitoes can be a problem, so take insect repellent.

• *Ginès Information Centre, Pont-de-Gau, Map A4, Open 9:30am–6pm daily*
• *Parc Ornithologique, Pont-de-Gau, Map A4, open 10am–sunset daily, Adm €5.50*
• *Musée Camarguais, Mas du Pont de Rousty, Map A4, Open Apr–Sep: 9:15am–5:45pm daily, Oct–Mar: 10am–4:45pm Wed–Mon, Adm €4.50*
• *Musée Baroncelli, rue Victor Hugo, Les-Saintes-Maries-de-la-Mer, Map A4, Open 10am–noon, 2–6pm daily, Adm €1.50*
• *Nature Information Centre, La Capelière, Map A4, Open 9am–6pm daily, Adm €3.00*
• *Château d'Avignon, Les Saintes-Maries-de-la-Mer, Map A4, Open Apr–Nov: guided tours 10am–5pm Adm €3.00*

Top 10 Sights

1. Ginès Information Centre
2. Parc Ornithologique du Pont-de-Gau
3. Eglise de Notre-Dame
4. Musée Camarguais
5. Domaine de Méjanes
6. The Salt Pans
7. Plage de Beauduc
8. Les-Saintes-Maries-de-la-Mer
9. Nature Information Centre
10. Château d'Avignon

1 Ginès Information Centre

A good place to start, at Pont-de-Gau, to understand the Camargue's exceptional natural environment. Displays explain aspects such as dune vegetation *(below)* and a panoramic window looks over local birdlife in the wild.

2 Parc Ornithologique du Pont-de-Gau

Next door to the information centre is this splendid bird park. Aviaries dotted around two acres of marshland house birds that are difficult to spot in the wild.

3 Eglise de Notre-Dame

The look-out tower of the little fortified church in Les-Saintes-Maries-de-la-Mer *(above)* served as a refuge against Saracen incursions from the 15th century *(see p32)*.

4 Musée Camarguais

A converted sheep barn in Mas du Pont de Rousty is a fine setting for an excellent little museum dealing with the interaction of man and nature in the Camargue.

5 Domaine de Méjanes

On the banks of Vaccarès lagoon, tourist train trips travel through local flora and fauna and, on Sundays, there are bull-game spectaculars.

For more areas of natural beauty in Provence See pp40–41

The Camargue

6 The Salt Pans

6 The largest salt pans in Europe *(above)*, in the southeast of the Camargue region, cover 26,000 acres and produce 800,000 tonnes of salt a year. See them shining in a red glow from the sun from a viewing point set up just south of Salin-de-Giraud.

9 Nature Information Centre

The HQ of the Camargue National Nature Reserve of the Vaccarès lagoon and surrounding area is in La Capelière, and has well-presented information on eco-systems and climate. Nature trails and observation posts let you put your new knowledge to the test.

10 Château d'Avignon

Here's evidence that existence isn't always a struggle in the Camargue. Surrounded by lovely grounds, the chateau outside Les-Saintes-Maries-de-la-Mer boasts the decoration of its 19th-century owners.

Camargue Bulls and Horses

The liveliest of the lithe Camargue bulls star in the *course Camarguaise* bull-running games, which take place in village arenas and on the streets. Camargue farmers also raise the larger fighting bulls for *corridas* in Spain and southern France. The Camargue horses which carry the *gardians* (cowboys) as they work only turn white as they reach adulthood. They are born almost black.

7 Plage de Beauduc

7 The beach at the end of the world. Its wild atmosphere has a hint of civilization, with shacks and cabins, two of which are fish restaurants.

8 Les-Saintes-Maries-de-la-Mer

The tiny main street and belltowers *(left)* of this old village seethe with crowds and colour in summer, but its seaside charm remains intact. It also contains the Musée Baroncelli, a slightly old-fashioned but interesting collection covering Camargue animal life and folklore.

TOP 10 Vaison-la-Romaine

Vaison is a delightful town which is made all the more fascinating by its fine array of Roman relics, including a graceful single-arched bridge that miraculously survived the devastating floods of the Ouvèze River in 1992. The Romans named the town Vasio Vocontiorum and it flourished under their rule for four centuries, but with the collapse of the empire, Vaison was gradually buried by sand deposited by the flood-prone river. It was rebuilt in the Middle Ages, but it wasn't until 1907 that archaeologists began to rediscover the Roman city.

3 Théâtre Antique
The theatre *(above)* is a dazzling display of Roman building skill, with 34 semi-circular rows of stone benches ascending to a columned portico.

Remains, House with the Silver Bust

🅾 The modern area of Vaison is filled with numerous, chic pavement cafés.

✔ Wear comfortable shoes, a sun hat and carry a bottle of water – especially in high summer.

• Map C2
• Office du Tourisme, pl du Chanoine Sautel, 04 90 36 02 11
• Roman ruins, Puymin and Musée Theo Desplans: pl du Chanoine, Sautel; Open Mar–Oct: 9:30am–12:30pm, 2–6pm daily, Nov–Feb: 10am–noon, 2–4:30pm Wed–Mon; Adm €6.00

Top 10 Sights
1 Puymin
2 Maison des Messii
3 Théâtre Antique
4 Nymphaeum
5 Portico of Pompey
6 Musée Theo Desplans
7 House with the Dolphin
8 House with the Silver Bust
9 Haute Ville and Pont Romain
10 Château

1 Puymin
This district *(below)* was the most important part of town in Roman times, containing the *praetorium* (courthouse), theatre, temples and shops. A broad road runs from the theatre to the main gate.

2 Maison des Messii
The House of the Messii must once have been the home of one of the town's most important families. Re-erected columns and foundations of an atrium, baths, temple to household gods, dining room and living rooms can still be seen.

4 Nymphaeum
The Nymphaeum was a rectangular sacred pool and fountain, covered by a roof supported by four columns. Traces of the building still remain, as does the sacred spring which provided the water supply. The area is now used as an open-air theatre.

For more Roman sights in Provence See pp30–31

5 Portico of Pompey

The impressive portico built by the family of Caesar's great rival Pompey is a massive, 65-m (210-ft) array of columns which originally surrounded an inner garden. Built around AD 20, it was demolished during the 5th century. Copies of statues *(right)* found on the site now stand in niches – the originals are preserved in the nearby museum.

8 House with the Silver Bust

Also named for a statue found here and now on show in the museum, the ruins of this once gracious villa, with its mosaic floors and paved hallway, are enhanced by copies of statues found here and elsewhere on the site.

9 Haute Ville and Pont Romain

Vaison's 2,000-year-old Roman bridge connects the upper town on the south bank with the north bank of the Ouvèze. The prettily restored old quarter *(below)*, with its 17th-century town houses, courtyards and fountains, is ringed by ramparts and entered through a massive, 14th-century stone gateway.

10 Château

At the highest point of the old town stands a dramatic, part-ruined castle *(left)*, built in 1160 by the Count of Toulouse. Three main wings and a formidable keep tower surround an inner courtyard.

6 Musée Théo Desplans

A muscular, life-size marble nude of the Emperor Hadrian, a statue of his empress Sabina, a gorgeous silver bust found at the Villasse site, and a six-seater public latrine are among the more interesting archaeological finds in this excellent museum.

7 House with the Dolphin

The House with the Dolphin was named after the marble statue of Cupid riding a dolphin which once stood here – it is now in the museum. The 2nd-century villa had a façade supported by 18 columns.

Abbaye de Sénanque

Surrounded by the purple lavender fields of the Luberon, the grey stone façade of the lovely Abbaye de Sénanque emanates tranquillity, but its past is anything but peaceful. Founded in 1148, Sénanque's golden age was the 13th century, when its ownership of several local farms brought new wealth. But in 1544 it was torched by the heretic Vaudois (see p118), in 1580 it was stricken by the plague, and by the 17th century only two monks were left in the crumbling building. The French Revolution and the anti-monastic laws of the 19th century were equally unkind, but since the 1970s, the abbey's fortunes have been restored by the patronage of the Association des Amis de Sénanque, and five monks now live here permanently.

Dormitory, Abbaye de Sénanque

The most striking approach to Sénanque is from Gordes, with a perfect panorama of the abbey as the road descends into the craggy valley in which Sénanque stands.

- Map C3
- 04 90 72 05 72
- Open Feb–Oct: 10am–noon, 2–6pm daily; Nov–Jan: 2–5pm daily
- Adm €4.00

Top 10 Features

1. Cloister
2. Refectory
3. Nave and Transept
4. Apse
5. Calefactory
6. Tomb of Seigneur de Venasque
7. Dormitory
8. Chapterhouse
9. Channels
10. Lavender Gardens

1 Cloister

The dove-grey limestone columns of the cloister *(below)*, decorated with delicate carvings of leaves, flowers and vines, are superb works of craftsmanship, dating from between 1180 and 1220.

2 Refectory

The Vaudois, would-be reformers of the Catholic church, attacked Sénanque and partly destroyed it in 1544. The refectory was rebuilt in the 17th century and has now been restored in its original style.

3 Nave and Transept

The barrel-vaulted nave and aisles of Sénanque are five bays long, and three stone steps lead from the nave to the square crossing, with its eight-sided dome. One of four altars is original.

4 Apse

The three windows of the raised, semi-circular apse symbolize the Holy Trinity.

For more places of worship in Provence **See pp32–3**

Calefactory
5 The calefactory *(above)* is symbolic of St Bernard's injunctions against luxury: this one heated room enabled monks to read and write without freezing.

Dormitory
7 The monks' dormitory is a huge, vaulted space, paved with flagstones which have been polished by centuries of use *(right)*. Arched windows at regular intervals along its walls and two large, circular windows at each end make the room light and airy.

Channels
9 The Cistercians came to this plateau seeking isolation, and built their abbey next to the region's only river, the Senancole. They channelled the water to flow through and under the abbey, providing sanitation, and irrigation for the gardens.

Lavender Gardens
10 The Abbaye de Sénanque is surrounded by fields of vivid purple lavender *(left)* which make a spectacular setting for the buildings in summer.

St Bernard and the Cistercians

With their complete lack of decoration or comfort, Provence's most outstanding Romanesque monasteries, Sénanque, Silvacane *(see p72)* and Le Thoronet *(see p77)*, reflect the austere ideals of the Cistercian order, founded in 1098 by St Bernard, abbot of Cîteaux. Rejecting the ostentatious luxury of the powerful Benedictine order, St Bernard advocated a rigorous and pure monastic life within simple, yet graceful and harmonious buildings.

Tomb of the Seigneur de Venasque
6 In a corner of the east arm of the transept, a small tombstone marks the grave of the 13th-century Lord of Venasque, the abbey's former patron.

Chapterhouse
8 The walls of the square chapterhouse, the abbey's assembly room, are lined with stone seats *(left)*. Here the monks sat each day to hear the abbot read a chapter from the Rule of St Bernard or a sermon from the Bible.

Casino de Monte Carlo

A magnificent belle époque extravaganza, Monte Carlo's Casino was designed in 1878 by Charles Garnier, architect of the Paris opera house. With its commanding position and dazzling views of Monaco, it is impressive enough from the outside. But within it is truly dazzling: a veritable temple to luck, luxury and ostentatious self-indulgence, haunted by the phantoms of royal and aristocratic gamblers including the Prince of Wales (later King Edward VII), Grand Duke Nicholas of Russia, and many more. The stage of the Salle Garnier attracted artistic talents such as the great ballet choreographers, Diaghilev and Nijinsky. Modern slot machines and video poker screens look decidedly out of place amid these grand surroundings.

Façade, Casino de Monte Carlo

🕐 If you want to gamble, ignore the roulette wheel and head straight for the blackjack table. It's the only game where the odds, ever so slightly, favour the player, not the casino.

- Pl du Casino, Monte Carlo, Monaco
- Map H3
- 00 377 92 16 20 00
- www.casino-monte-carlo.com
- Salle Europe (roulette): Open noon–late daily, Adm €7.60; English Club (blackjack, roulette): Open 4pm–late daily, Adm €15.00; Salle des Palmiers: Open Jul–mid-Sep 10pm–late daily, Adm €15.00.
- No admission under 21, passport or ID card required, jacket and tie required.

Top 10 Features
1. Atrium
2. Salle Garnier
3. Salon Blanc
4. Salon Rose
5. Renaissance Hall
6. Salle Europe
7. Salles Privées
8. Salle des Palmiers
9. Jardins de Casino
10. Café de Paris

1 Atrium
Paved in marble, the vast entrance hall is surrounded by 28 Ionic columns. The atrium links the casino with the Salle Garnier, and its grandeur gives a hint of what awaits within.

2 Salle Garnier
Named after the architect, the concert hall *(below)* is lavishly turned out in red and gold, its walls adorned with frescoes and encrusted with bas-reliefs.

3 Salon Blanc
The wall painting in the White Room, *Graces of Florence*, depicts three muses said to represent 19th-century French courtesans, Cleo de Merode, Liane de Pougy and Otero.

4 Salon Rose
The ceiling is the most noteworthy feature of the casino's smoking room. It is decorated with voluptuous, cigar-smoking female nudes whose gaze, according to legend, follows you around the room.

6 Salle Europe

The opulent Salle Europe, where roulette is again the featured game, is lit by eight huge chandeliers of glittering Bohemian crystal *(left)*.

7 Salles Privées

The Salle Médecin, Salle de l'Empire and Salle Touzet are the casino's private rooms. Behind closed doors the high rollers gather, in surroundings of gilded mahogany.

9 Jardins de Casino

Opposite the casino are the magnificent flower gardens, immaculate lawns and lily pools of the Casino Gardens *(above)*, sloping up towards Monaco's most exclusive shopping area *(see p99)*.

10 Café de Paris

King Edward VII was a regular customer to the *belle époque* café in front of the casino, first known as the Café Divan. In the 1930s, while retaining its original façade, it was transformed into an Art Deco triumph and was lovingly renovated again in 1988 *(see p102)*.

The Man who Broke the Bank

Many visitors to the casino still follow the superstitious tradition of stroking the knee of the horse – part of an equestrian statue of Louis XIV – in the foyer of the Hôtel de Paris, to bring luck. Luckiest of all was Charles Wells, who, in 1891, raked in one million gold francs in a three-day winning streak, then won three million more on a second visit. The event inspired the song "The Man Who Broke the Bank at Monte Carlo". But his luck failed in the end, and on a third visit the casino cleaned him out.

5 Renaissance Hall

This large room filled with roulette tables *(below)* is the main gaming room. Its *belle époque* finery imitates the high style of the Italian Renaissance.

8 Salle des Palmiers

In summer, gaming moves to the Salle des Palmiers, a contemporary building with fine views of the sea from its lovely bars and terraces.

Left **Ancient village huts, Gordes** Right **Roman mosaic, Vaison-la-Romaine**

🔟 Moments in History

1 Early Settlers
Carvings in the Grotte d'Observatoire in Monaco and paintings in the Grotte Cosquer near Marseille date from as far back as 1 million BC. Between 2500 and 2000 BC, dwellers in the Vallée des Merveilles *(see p105)* left behind carvings of beasts and human figures.

2 Foundation of Aix
In 123 BC the Phoenician Greeks, settled in Marseille since 600 BC, asked for Roman help against the invading Celtic tribes inland. After defeating the Celts, the Romans founded Aquae Sextia (Aix) in the area *(see pp14–15)*.

3 Advent of Christianity
In AD 40 St Honorat brought Christianity to Provence, founding the first monastery on Ile de Lérins. Camarguais legend, however, claims Christianity was brought here by Mary Magdalene herself *(see p60)*.

4 Franks and Saracens
With the fall of the Roman Empire in AD 476 Provence was pillaged by barbarians, eventually coming under the rule of the Franks. From the 8th century the coasts were harried by Moorish pirates who gave their name to the Massif des Maures. They were finally defeated in 974 by Guillaume le Libérateur, Count of Arles.

5 Dawn of a Dynasty
In 1297 François Grimaldi, a supporter of the papacy in the Guelph-Ghibelline feuds which beset 13th-century Italy, seized Monaco and its castle to found the dynasty which still rules there today.

6 The Avignon Papacy
Pope Clement V relocated to Avignon in 1309 to escape strife-torn Rome, the first of a succession of nine French pontiffs who were to reside in the Provençal town. In 1348 Clement VI bought the city and Avignon remained the seat of the papacy until 1377 *(see pp8–9)*.

Monastère Fortifié, built as protection against Saracen pirates

Papal Avignon

7 Union with France

In 1486 King René of Naples, the last of the Anjou dynasty who ruled Provence from 1246, died without issue, and most of the region became part of France. Nice and the Alpes Maritimes, however, remained part of the Kingdom of Savoy, before finally passing to France in 1860.

8 Plague and War

In the second half of the 16th century religious strife erupted in the Luberon between reforming Vaudois (Huguenot) factions and conservative Catholic forces. The plague of 1580 added to the region's woes.

9 La Marseillaise

When the French Revolution erupted in 1789, the people of Marseille were among its staunchest supporters, marching to a tune that became known as La Marseillaise, now France's national anthem.

10 Resistance and Liberation

After the Nazi invasion of 1940, Provence was ruled by the collaborationist Vichy government, until it was occupied by Germany in 1942. Guerrilla fighters in the *maquis* (scrubland) resisted the Occupation. On 15 August 1944, Allied troops landed, liberating Provence after two weeks of fighting.

Top 10 Figures in History

1 Julius Caesar
Caesar besieged Marseille after its citizens sided with his rival Pompey in 49 BC.

2 François Grimaldi
Grimaldi disguised his soldiers as monks in order to seize Monaco in 1297.

3 The Anti-pope
When the papacy returned to Rome, French cardinals elected Robert de Genève as Pope Clement VII, creating a split in the Church until 1417.

4 Petrarch
The Italian Renaissance poet (1304–74), who lived in Avignon, was a critic of the ostentatious French papacy.

5 Nostradamus
Born in St-Rémy-de-Provence, the scholar (1503–66) published his book of prophecies in 1555.

6 Napoleon Bonaparte
Bonaparte landed at Golfe-Juan on 1 March 1815 to regain his empire, only to be defeated at Waterloo.

7 Louis-Auguste Blanqui
Born in Puget-Théniers in 1805, the socialist was one of the leaders of the revolutionary Paris Commune of 1871.

8 Jacques Cousteau
Toulon-based naval officer Cousteau perfected the aqualung in the 1940s, pioneering the sport of scuba diving.

9 Antoine de St-Exupéry
The aircraft of the French author and pilot vanished in 1944 while on a reconnaissance flight over Provence.

10 Brigitte Bardot
Sex icon and film star Bardot became the symbol of St-Tropez in the 1960s.

Left and centre **Roman amphitheatre, Orange** Right **Arc de Triomphe, Cavaillon**

🔟 Roman Sights

1 Arles
Remnants of Provence's most important Roman settlement can still be seen around this lovely town *(see pp12–13)*.

2 Vaison-la-Romaine
Another Roman gem, discovered in 1907 *(see pp22–3)*.

3 Parc de la Colline St-Eutrope, Orange
One of the best preserved theatres from the Roman empire, built during the reign of Augustus (c.27–25 BC), is the highlight of the Parc de la Colline St-Eutrope. Nearby, a triumphal arch decorated with relief carvings commemorates Julius Caesar's victories over Gaul *(see p117)*.

4 Les Antiques de Glanum
Twin temples, a Roman forum, baths and a fortified gate can be seen at Glanum, near St-Rémy, which also reveals traces of a 4th-century Greek settlement. Another triumphal arch (10 BC) marks more Gallic victories *(see p71)*.

Triumphal arch, Glanum

5 La Trophée des Alpes
This majestic Roman monument, built from local white stone, was erected in 6 BC to mark the boundary between Italy and Gaul and to honour Augustus's Gallic conquests. Towering over the small village of La Turbie, high above Monte Carlo, with breathtaking views of the Riviera, it still has the power to impress *(see p107)*.

La Trophée des Alpes

6 Les Arènes de Fréjus
Like other large Roman arenas in Provence, the amphitheatre at Fréjus *(see p77)*, which can seat up to 10,000 people, is still used regularly for bullfights and classical music concerts. Extensively restored, it was originally built in the 1st–2nd centuries AD. Nearby are parts of the original Roman wall, including gate towers.
🅢 Rue Vadon • Map F4 • Open 10am–noon, 1:30–5:30pm Wed–Mon • Adm

7 Arc de Triomphe, Cavaillon

This twin-arched triumphal gate, lavishly adorned with carved vines and dramatic Corinthian columns, was built during the reign of the Emperor Augustus, in the 1st century AD. There are other interesting Roman finds in the town's archaeological museum. ✎ Map C3

8 Arc de Triomphe, Carpentras

Yet another monumental arch in celebration of Augustus's victories over the rebellious Gauls stands in the courtyard of the Palais de Justice in Carpentras (see p119), where it was originally the main gate through the Roman walls. Its carvings, much worn away, still show Gallic prisoners in chains. ✎ Map C3

9 Roche Taillée, Mons

This village aqueduct cut deep into solid rock is an impressive example of Roman civil engineering and an indication of how highly the Romans valued civilized comforts such as a reliable supply of running water. Those comforts unfortunately vanished with the fall of the Empire and were not regained until the 19th century. ✎ Map F4

Roche Taillée aqueduct

10 Temple of Apollo, Riez

The four Corinthian columns of the 1st-century-AD temple to Apollo, standing tall and alone among fields just outside Riez on the Valensole plateau, are all that remain of the once prosperous Roman settlement of Reia Apollinaris. Eight ancient pillars, perhaps scavenged from another Roman building, are now in the early Christian church nearby, which dates from the 4th–5th century BC and is one of the oldest surviving churches in France. ✎ Map E3

Left **Matisse drawing, Chapelle de la Rosarie** Right **Abbaye de Montmajour**

🔟 Places of Worship

1 Eglise St-Trophime, Arles

St-Trophime's elegant interior and Romanesque carving make it the most attractive of all Provençal churches. It's also one of the oldest – a church stood here as early as AD 450. In the 11th century the church was re-built and dedicated to St Trophime *(see p13)*. ✪ Pl de la République • Map B4 • Open Apr–Sep: 9am–7pm daily; Oct–Mar: 10am–4:30pm daily • Free

2 Notre-Dame-de-Beaulieu, Cucuron

A harmonious blend of Roman-esque and Gothic, with a barrel-vaulted nave and rib-vaulted apse, this church dates from the 14th century. Elaborate geometric patterns decorate the doorway. ✪ Map H4 • Open 9am–6pm daily • Free

3 Eglise de Notre-Dame, Les-Saintes-Maries-de-la-Mer

The belltower of this fortified church is a Camargue landmark. The church has lent its name to the capital of the region, and its sturdy walls offered villagers refuge from raiders and pirates. The most colourful sight is the carved boat with statues of the Virgin and Mary Magdalene. ✪ Map A4 • Open 8am–12:30pm, 2–7pm daily • Free

4 Abbaye de Montmajour

The extraordinary abbey of Montmajour was built on a rocky island amid the Rhône marshes. It was an important pilgrimage site and became wealthy on its sale of pardons for sins. The cloister is decorated with mythi-cal and Biblical scenes *(see p72)*.

5 Cathédrale, Fréjus

Constructed in the pink stone typical of Fréjus, the 13th-century cathedral has a beautiful Renaissance doorway. Its interior is dominated by superb pointed arches, and the cloister ceiling, with its scenes of the Apoca-lypse, is unique *(see p77)*.

6 Notre-Dame, Grasse

Fragonard's depiction of *Christ Washing the Disciples' Feet* is the main reason for visiting this 13th-century church. It also contains three striking religious works by Rubens, all painted in

Cathédrale, Fréjus

Rome in 1601: *The Crown of Thorns*, *The Crucifixion of Christ* and *The Deposition of St Helena*. ◈ Pl du Petit Puy • Map G3 • Open 8–11:30am, 2–6pm Mon–Sat, 2–6pm Sun • DA • Free

7 Chapelle des Pénitents Blancs, La Tour

Lively frescoes (1491) greet visitors to this simple chapel. They include scenes of the Last Judgment, with St Peter welcoming the virtuous to Heaven while the Devil leads the damned to Hell. Above is a Gothic portrayal of the Passion. ◈ Map D3 • Open 9:30am–12:30pm, 2:30–6pm daily • Free

Notre-Dame, Grasse

8 Notre-Dame de l'Assomption, Puget-Théniers

Built by the Knights Templar, the 13th-century parish church of this mountain village has a beautiful altarpiece, *Notre Dame de Secours* (1525) by Antoine Ronzen, and a reredos of the Passion carried out by Flemish craftsmen. ◈ Map G3 • Open 9:30am–12:30pm, 2:30–6pm daily • Free

9 Notre-Dame du Bourg, Digne-les-Bains

Lovely arched windows bring light into this striking former cathedral, probably built during the 13th century. Its west front is lavishly decorated with carved stonework. Inside, a pointed arch is pierced by a single window. ◈ Ave St-Jean de Chrisostome • Map E2 • Open 3–6pm daily • DA • Free

10 Chapelle de la Rosarie, St-Paul-de-Vence

The dazzling white interior walls of this little chapel are adorned with black line drawings of the Stations of the Cross. They are unmistakably the work of Henri Matisse *(see p36)*, who designed this serene building in 1949. ◈ Map G4 • Open 10–11:30am, 2:30–5:30pm Tue–Thu • Adm

Left **Mosaic, Musée Jean Cocteau** Right **Pierre-Auguste Renoir**

TOP 10 Art Galleries

1 Musée de l'Annonciade, St-Tropez

This museum tops Provence's list of superb art collections. Opened in 1955, it boasts works by Pierre Bonnard, Raoul Dufy, the pointillist Paul Signac and Charles Camoin, whose work *St-Tropez, la Place des Lices et le Café des Arts* (1925), is one of the most famous images of the town *(see p18)*. ◎ Pl Grammont, Vieux Port • Map F5 • Open Jun–Sep: 10am–noon, 3–7pm; Oct & Dec–May 10am–noon, 2–6pm Wed–Mon • Adm

2 Fondation Maeght, St-Paul-de-Vence

This small museum has a world-class array of modern art, including paintings by Léger, Bonnard and Chagall, sculpture by Miró and a mosaic pool by Braque *(see p105)*.

3 Musée Matisse, Nice

The most attractive collection in Nice, the Musée Matisse was founded in 1963, nine years after the painter's death, and is housed in the 17th-century Villa des Arènes. The collection includes sketches, paintings and bronze sculpture by the prolific artist, as well as some of his personal effects *(see p87)*.

4 Musée Picasso, Antibes

Housed in the Château Grimaldi, used as a studio by Picasso in 1946, the museum contains more than 50 of his paintings, sketches, prints and ceramics, as well as works by Léger and Miró *(see p93)*.

5 Musée Chagall, Nice

One of the jewels of Provence, this museum houses the world's largest collection of works by Marc Chagall, including 17 canvases from his Biblical Message series. The Biblical theme is continued in three stained-glass windows depicting the Creation *(see p88)*.

6 Musée Fernand Léger, Biot

Mosaics in primary colours, carried out to Léger's own design, identify this strikingly modern museum. The Cubist painter planned to build a studio here just before his death in 1955, and the museum contains more than 400 of his works *(see p105)*.

Marteau de Porte, Aristide Maillol, Musée de l'Annonciade

7 Musée Jean Cocteau, Menton

The multi-talented Jean Cocteau, a playwright, author and film director as well as artist and designer, converted this 17th-century fort

Musée Jean Cocteau

into his personal museum, donating tapestries, set designs and drawings to the collection.
🕲 *Quai de Monléon* • *Map H3* • *Open 10am–noon, 2–6pm Wed–Mon* • *Adm*

8 Musée d'Art Moderne et d'Art Contemporain, Nice

A dazzling work of contemporary architecture in its own right, with marble-faced towers and glass corridors, the contemporary art museum contains works by some of the 20th century's greatest avant-garde artists, including Andy Warhol *(see p87)*.

9 Musée des Beaux-Arts, Menton

Menton's museum of fine art is housed in the former summer palace of the Grimaldi princes of Monaco and has an extensive collection. High points include works by Utrillo, Dufy and the English painter Graham Sutherland. 🕲 *Palais Carnolès, 3 ave de la Madone* • *Map H3* • *Open 9am–5pm Wed–Mon* • *Adm* • *DA*

10 Musée Renoir, Cagnes-sur-Mer

Renoir's house at Les Collettes, where the painter came in hope that the climate would cure his rheumatism, houses 10 of his paintings, as well as works by Dufy and Bonnard *(see p94)*.

Top 10 Masterpieces of Provence

1 Café du Soir
Vincent van Gogh painted more than 300 canvases in the town of Arles *(see pp12–13)*. Café du Soir (1888) is one of the best known.

2 La Joie de Vivre
This 1946 work is one of Picasso's most important from his Antibes period.

3 La Partie de Campagne
Fernand Léger overlays bold colours on bold, comic-book outlines in this 1954 painting.

4 Nu Bleu IV
The 1952 work is among the best known of Matisse's blue paper cut-outs series.

5 St-Tropez, la Place des Lices et le Café des Arts
Charles Camoin evokes the St-Tropez of 1925.

6 L'Orage
Pointillist Paul Signac's 1895 work glowingly depicts St-Tropez harbour.

7 La Montagne Sainte-Victoire au Grand Pin
This 1887 painting is one of Cézanne's most renowned images of the Provence mountain *(see p15)*.

8 The Burning Bush
Nicolas Froment's 1476 triptych in the Cathédrale de St-Saveur *(see p14)* was commissioned by Provence's last king, René.

9 Jetée Promenade à Nice
Portraying an evening stroll on the esplanade, the 1928 work is Dufy at his colourful best.

10 Venus Victrix
One of Renoir's finest bronzes (1914) stands amid the olive groves at Les Collettes.

Left **Jetée d'Honfleur, Raoul Dufy** Right **Self Portrait, Pablo Picasso**

🔟 Painters in Provence

1 Paul Cézanne
Born in Aix, where he lived most of his life, Cézanne (1839–1906) painted hundreds of oil and watercolour scenes of his home town and the nearby Mont Sainte-Victoire *(see pp14–15)* in his own Post-Impressionist style. Better than any other painter, he captures the soul of Provence.

2 Vincent van Gogh
The Dutch master (1854–90) created hundreds of his vivid, powerful landscapes and self-portraits during his few years in Arles and St-Rémy. The sunshine of Provence changed the way Van Gogh saw light and colour.

3 Pablo Picasso
The driving force behind the Cubist movement, Picasso (1881–1973) was influenced by the sights and colours of Provence, where he lived in exile from his native Spain for much of his life. He learned to make ceramics from the potters of Vallauris and helped revive the craft *(see p100)*.

4 Henri Matisse
Matisse (1869–1954) lived in Nice from 1917 until his death. His earlier works were inspired by the vivid light and colours of the Riviera. During World War II he retreated to St-Paul-de-Vence, where he designed the unique Chapelle de la Rosarie, including its vestments and furnishings *(see p33)*.

5 Paul Signac
The masterful exponent of pointillist style, Signac (1863–1935) came to St-Tropez in 1892. He found, in the glittering reflection of sun on sea, the perfect subject for pointillism's technique of using a myriad of tiny rainbow dots to depict swathes or blocks of colour, giving an almost psychedelic effect.

6 Marc Chagall
The Russian-born painter (1887–1985) moved to St-Paul-de-Vence in 1949. His light-filled, almost childlike work was often inspired by Biblical themes and canvases from his Biblical Message series of paintings are displayed in the Musée Marc Chagall in Nice *(see p88)*.

La Montagne Sainte-Victoire, Paul Cézanne

For the Top 10 art galleries in Provence **See pp34–5**

Lilac Bush, Vincent van Gogh

7 Fernand Léger
Léger (1881–1955) is known for his strong Cubist paintings and his love of bold lines and pure primary colours. First a figurative painter, he worked in the Cubist style before returning to simplified, colourful painting that seems to echo poster or graphic art.

8 Yves Klein
Born in Iceland, Klein (1928–62) became one of the leading lights of the Nice School of new realists, who aimed to create art from everyday materials. His *Anthropométries*, in Nice's Musée d'Art Contemporain *(see p87)*, was created by three paint-covered nude women rolling over a huge white canvas.

9 Raoul Dufy
Dufy (1877–1963) embodies the values of the Fauvist school, with its revolutionary use of bright, intense colour. He found Nice the perfect background for his vivid work.

10 Paul Gigou
This realist painter (1834–71) painted sunny landscapes of his native Vaucluse, capturing the pure light of Provence's rugged hillsides. Among his best known works is *Deux Lavandières devant la Sainte-Victoire*, on display in the Musée Grobet-Labadie in Marseille *(see p66)*.

Top 10 Writers in Provence

1 Frédéric Mistral
This Nobel Prize-winner (1830–1914) wrote epic poems based on local lore.

2 Alexandre Dumas
Dumas (1802–70) used the Château d'If *(see p67)* as the grim backdrop to *The Count of Monte Cristo* (1845).

3 Victor Hugo
Hugo (1802–85) set the early chapters of his epic novel *Les Misérables* (1862) in Digne-les-Bains.

4 Albert Camus
This French author and existentialist (1913–60) wrote his autobiography at Lourmarin.

5 Alphonse Daudet
Daudet (1849–97) is best remembered for *Tartarin de Tarascon*, the tale of a Provençal bumpkin *(see p60)*.

6 Graham Greene
The English novelist (1914–91) retired to Nice, where he wrote *J'Accuse – the Dark Side of Nice* (1982).

7 F. Scott Fitzgerald
The US writer (1896–1940) stayed at Juan-les-Pins in 1926 to write his novel *Tender is the Night*.

8 Ernest Hemingway
Another US visitor to Provence, Hemingway (1898–1961) set *The Garden of Eden* in La Napoule.

9 Marcel Pagnol
The French author and film director (1895–1974) wrote *L'Eau des Collines* (1963), later filmed as *Jean de Florette* and *Manon des Sources*.

10 Colette
Colette (1873–1954) wrote charmingly of St-Tropez in *La Naissance du Jour* (1928).

Left **Bormes-les-Mimosas** Centre **Fontaine-de-Vaucluse** Right **St-Paul-de-Vence**

🔟 Provence Villages

1 Moustiers-Ste-Marie
At the entrance to the Verdon gorges *(see pp10–11)*, Moustiers hangs like a pendant from the rock-face soaring above *(see p112)*. The glorious tangle of vaulted streets, tiny squares and tiled roofs is divided by rushing streams. Up above, tucked against the rocks, is the Notre-Dame-de-Beauvoir chapel *(see p11)*. The village is also celebrated for its pottery.

Chapel, Les-Baux-de-Provence

2 Les-Baux-de-Provence
Emerging dramatically from its crag on the edge of the Alpilles hills, Les-Baux was home to one of the finest courts in medieval Provence. Abandoned for centuries, the ruined castle and labyrinthine streets now throb with summer tourists. But the site remains majestic, the atmosphere lively and the views over mountains and plains quite breathtaking *(see p71)*.

3 St-Paul-de-Vence
St-Paul was a farming community living quietly within its medieval surroundings and 16th-century walls until the 1920s. Then it was discovered by the Côte d'Azur artistic community (Picasso, Matisse, Léger) and has been fashionable ever since, with good reason. Both artists and tourists find the tiny streets, ramparts and church remains utterly charming *(see p108)*.

4 Fontaine-de-Vaucluse
The "*fontaine*" is actually Europe's most powerful natural spring – it pumps out 2.5 million cubic m (55 million gallons) of water a day, giving birth to the River Sorgue. It's a spectacular setting for a lovely village, made even more romantic by its association with the Italian love poet, Petrarch, who lived here in the 14th century *(see p118)*.

5 Bormes-les-Mimosas
This delightful village seems to tumble down the hillside, its jumble of steep alleys, hidden corners and stone houses overcome with flowers – the village name tells no lies. Climb to the top and the views to the sea from the ruined medieval castle are splendid *(see p79)*.

6 Roussillon
Roussillon is perched beautifully above a quite extraordinary landscape. The mining of ochre and subsequent erosion have

Provence's Top 10

sculpted the red-and-gold earth into cliffs, canyons and weird shapes. Villagers have applied the local product to their houses, to enchanting effect *(see p123)*.

7 Séguret
Encircling its hillside like a belt, Séguret stares out from the edges of the Dentelles de Montmirail mountains across the nearby wine plain. It's an almost impossibly pretty spot of tiny, pedestrianized streets, medieval edifices and contemporary artists and artisans *(see p123)*.

8 Cassis
Cassis is overseen by France's highest coastal cliffs, whose scale reinforces the intimacy of the narrow little harbour and old town centre down below. Tourists crowd the beaches – the best bathing is in the creeks to the west – but Cassis remains a fishing port, and well retains its authenticity *(see p72)*.

9 Sisteron
At the northern gateway to Provence, Sisteron's minuscule vaulted streets and unexpected staircases climb the vast sentinel

Pâtisserie, Sisteron

rock overlooking the River Durance. It's a harsh setting for a village with a strong past. Up top, the 14th-century citadel was all but impregnable and now affords unbeatable views over the rugged landscape *(see p111)*.

10 Roquebrune-Cap-Martin
A winning partnership of the sort only found on the Côte d'Azur. Beneath Roquebrune are the grandiose *belle époque* villas of the super-rich on the Cap-Martin peninsula. Up above are the winding streets, vaulted passages and 10th-century chateau of the original village *(see p95)*.

Left **Camargue cowboy** Right **Les Alpilles**

Areas of Natural Beauty

1 The Camargue
A landscape of lagoons, marshes, wild bulls and Europe's only cowboys *(see pp20–21)*.

2 Parc National du Mercantour
Mercantour National Park, sprawling over 700 sq km (270 sq miles), is one of Europe's largest and its rocky slopes are home to rare species including chamois, ibex, moufflon and marmot. Golden eagles and the rare lammergeier vulture soar above the peaks *(see p105)*. ❧ Map G2

Mont Ventoux

3 Parc Naturel Régional du Luberon
The Luberon region contains a wide range of habitats. The northern mountains are wild and exposed, while the central massif shelters the southern slopes, creating a gentler environment. Moorland, cedar forest, chalk hills and deep river gorges shelter wild boar, eagles, owls and beavers *(see p117)*.

4 Parc National de Port-Cros
Port-Cros is the smallest of the Îles d'Hyères, and the national park protects the delightful island and 18 sq km (7 sq miles) of sea around it from the development that has overtaken so much of the coast. On land, it shelters beautiful butterflies and rare sea birds, and there is excellent scuba diving and snorkelling *(see p83)*. ❧ Map E6

5 Mont Ventoux
The lonely peak of Mont Ventoux, at 1,910 m (6,260 ft), seems to guard the gateway to the region. Bare of trees, its higher slopes are known as the *désert de pierre* (stone desert) and are snow-covered from December to April. It has featured in the Tour de France, and even the strongest cyclists dread the treacherous ascent *(see p119)*.

6 Les Alpilles
The chalky hills of the "Little Alps" rise no higher than 500 m (1,640 ft) but display an arid beauty. This miniature sierra stretches for 24 km (15 miles) between the rivers Rhône and Durance, and the GR6 hiking trail which crosses it is one of the finest walks in Provence *(see p73)*. ❧ Map B4

7 Gorges du Cians and Gorges du Dalius
High in the mountains of Haute-Provence and the Alpes-Maritimes, the parallel canyons

 For walks in Provence **See p57**

of the Gorges du Cians and the Gorges du Dalius are awesome ravines, carved by icy fast-flowing streams running down from wine-red cliffs. The main landmark is the Gardienne des Gorges, a huge boulder shaped like a woman's head, standing at the north end of the Gorges du Dalius *(see p106)*.

Farmers, Massif des Maures

8 Gorges du Loup

The clifftop village of Gourdon, set in rugged limestone country, stands above the dramatic Gorges du Loup, the most accessible of the gorges and canyons that slash through this craggy landscape. The Loup stream plunges over high cascades and has carved deep potholes such as the Saut du Loup ("Wolf's Leap") *(see p106)*.

9 Massif des Maures

Thickly wooded with forests of cork and holm oak, pine, myrtle and sweet chestnut, the dramatic Massif des Maures is wild, hilly and sparsely inhabited,

even though it is only a stone's throw from the busy coastal hotspots. It is home to France's only surviving wild tortoises, and makes a welcome change from crowded beaches *(see p79)*.

10 Réserve Géologique de Haute-Provence

If dinosaurs and fossils are your thing, this park in the limestone country around Digne is the place to head for. It's the largest of its kind in Europe, covering 1,900 sq km (730 sq miles) of rock, rich in fossils from ancient seas and tropical forests dating back 300 million years. Ⓢ *Map F2*

Left **Summer on the Riviera** Right **Hillside view over the Riviera**

Beaches in Provence

1 Notre Dame Beach, Ile de Porquerolles

No cars are allowed on the island, so it's a walk or cycle-ride along the rocky, 3-km (2-mile) track from the port to the loveliest beach in France (see p83). Pine-fringed, it boasts white, calm waters, no commerce and few people. Your private slice of paradise. ✆ Map E6

Pampelonne Beach, St-Tropez

2 Pampelonne Beach, St-Tropez

Everyone has his or her "place" on St-Trop's largest beach. Famous beach clubs cater to the super-rich and glamorous, to nudists, to gays, as well as to everyday families. The 5-km (3-mile) sandy stretch across the headland from the town also has extensive public areas. There's space in which to escape the crowds and appreciate natural beauty (see p19). ✆ Map F5

3 Calanque d'En-Vau, Cassis

"Calanques" are creeks formed where the chalk cliffs between Cassis and Marseille

plunge to the sea. En-Vau is the prettiest and one of the more accessible – a mere 90-minute walk from the nearest Cassis car park. It's worth it. At the foot of the white, pine-clad rocks, the setting of sand and luminous sea is intimate, wild and quite unforgettable (see p66).

4 Elephant Beach, Le Lavandou

Le Lavandou has a total of 12 beaches, covering the full seaside spectrum, from the great sandy stretch of the Grande Plage to the nudist creek of Rossignol. Most appealing of all, however, is l'Eléphant. The approach is only by sea or by scrambling over rocks, a feature which usually ensures relative tranquillity. ✆ Map F5

Le Lavandou beach

Provence's Top 10

42

For beach activities in Provence **See p83 & p98**

5 Calanque de Figuerolles, La Ciotat

Steps on the eastern edge of town lead down to this extra-ordinary creek. On either side are cliffs, while further back are terraces of fig-trees and pines. Out front, the blue sea laps around weird rock formations and onto the pebble shore. A world unto itself. ◎ *Map D5*

6 La Garoupe Beach, Cap-d'Antibes

Between them, Antibes and Juan-les-Pins have 25 km (16 miles) of coast and 48 beaches, slotted into rocky creeks or opening out into sandy expanses. The prettiest is La Garoupe, on an inlet of the peninsula. It's highly fashionable and, in summer, very crowded – but with good reason. ◎ *Map G4*

7 Agay Beach, St-Raphaël

As the red rocks of the Esterel hills tumble into the clear blue sea, they give the coast around St-Raphaël an untamed allure. The small creeks are enticing; equally alluring, but bigger, sandier and more acces-sible, is the Bay of Agay – perfect for families *(see p98)*.

8 St-Honorat Beaches, Iles de Lérins

A short ferry ride leads from the crowds of Cannes to this island owned by Cistercian monks. The presence of the monastery seems to discourage more brazen holidaymakers so the pretty rock outcrops and tiny beaches remain calm and, unusually for Provence, under-populated. ◎ *Map G4*

9 St-Aygulf Beach

Long, wide, sandy and safe, the main beach at St-Aygulf, near Fréjus *(see p77)*, has the additional advantage of being in a Nature Preservation Area. This protects the Etangs de Villepey – great, wild, freshwater lagoons on the other side of the road, where 217 different bird species have been noted. A beautiful setting. ◎ *Map B5*

Camargue beach

10 Piémançon Beach, The Camargue

This is the beach beyond civilization. You must thread around salt-flats and lagoons before arriving at the flat, exposed sands. Life is a little rugged, but ideal for wilder beach elements. ◎ *Map B5*

Left **Port-Cros, Iles d'Hyères** Right **Ste-Marguérite, Iles de Lérins**

🔟 Offshore Islands

1 Porquerolles, Iles d'Hyères
The largest of the French
Riviera islands is the car-free idyll
of Porquerolles. Hire a bike or
explore on foot to appreciate this
paradise of vineyards, olive
groves, scented forests and
glorious beaches. ◈ Map E6 • Ferry
from La Tour-Fondue, near Giens

2 Port Cros, Iles d'Hyères
Now a national park, the
smallest and most mountainous
of the Hyères isles is dense with
pine woods and oaks. Paths lead
up to clifftops with dramatic
views. La Palud is the best
beach. ◈ Map F6 • Ferry from Hyères

3 Le Levant, Iles d'Hyères
Although 90 per cent of this
island is a French Navy missile
base, the other 10 per cent is a
naturist colony. Clothes must be
worn in the village but not
beyond. ◈ Map F6 • Ferry from Hyères

4 Iles de Frioul
The islands of Ratonneau
and Pomègues guard Marseille
harbour (see p65). Beyond Port
Frioul, white rocks ruggedly con-
ceal little beaches. The diving
here is renowned. ◈ Map C5 • Ferry
from Vieux Port, Marseille

5 Ile d'If
This prison island is most
famous as the place from which
the fictional Count of Monte
Cristo escaped (see p37). You
may even visit the "Count's
dungeon". ◈ Map C5 • Ferry from
Vieux Port, Marseille

6 Ste-Marguérite, Iles de Lérins
Ste-Marguérite offers woods of
pine and eucalyptus and little
stony beaches. In 1687 the Man
In The Iron Mask was imprisoned
in the island's fort (see p60).
◈ Map G4 • Ferry from Cannes harbour

Iles d'Hyères coastline

Fort, Ste-Marguerite

7 St-Honorat, Iles de Lérins

A smaller version of Ste-Marguérite, St-Honorat has been run by monks almost continually since the 5th century. The 11th-century fortified monastery is a must-see. ✆ *Map G4 • Ferry from Cannes harbour • Fortified monastery: Open Jul–Aug: 10am–noon, 2:30–6:30pm; Sep–Jun: 9am–4pm daily; Adm (Jul–Aug only)*

8 Iles des Embiez

The larger of two islands developed for tourism by French drinks magnate Paul Ricard, Embiez is a delight. Holiday development has been merged into the landscape around the port, leaving the rest of the island untouched, with its creeks, woods and salt marshes . ✆ *Map D5 • Ferry from Le Brusc, near Six-Fours-les-Plages*

9 Bendor

Embiez's baby brother has a tiny harbour and beaches – you can do the tour in 20 minutes. But the tourist development is as sensitive as on Embiez, marrying the landscape extremely naturally. ✆ *Map D5 • Ferry from Bandol*

10 Ile Verte

"Verte" refers to the island's greenery, notably the trees topping the steep cliffs. Billed as "one of the last virgin islands of the Mediterranean coast", the islet has tiny creeks and beaches. ✆ *Map D5 • Ferry from La Ciotat old port*

Top 10 Island Activities

1 Cycling

On Porquerolles and Embiez, cycle the forest paths to creeks and beaches. Bikes are hired from the port areas.

2 Scuba-diving, Port Cros

A guided underwater "trail" gives close-ups of marine life. Equipment for hire. ✆ *National Park Office • 04 94 01 40 72*

3 Fort Ste-Agathe, Porquerolles

The fort has exhibitions on marine life. ✆ *Open May–Sep: 10am–noon, 2–5:30pm • Adm*

4 Diving, Embiez

Courses held in water rich with marine life. ✆ *Centre de Plongée • 04 94 34 12 78*

5 Lighthouse Walk, Porquerolles

A 90-minute round trip to one of the finest lighthouses.

6 Fort de l'Estissac, Port Cros

Exhibits on sea life. ✆ *Open May–Sep: 10am–12:30pm, 1:30–5:30pm • Adm*

7 Aquascope Bubble, Embiez

Glass "bubble" suspended under water allows close encounters of a marine kind. ✆ *Open Apr–Sep • Adm*

8 Sailing, Bendor

Sailing classes all year round. ✆ *Club Nautique de Bendor • 04 94 29 52 91*

9 Vallon de la Solitude Walk, Port Cros

A 2-hour walk through shady forest to the Fort de la Vigie.

10 Wine and Spirits Exhibition, Bendor

Attractively odd display of 8,000 bottles from 51 countries. ✆ *Open Apr–Sep: 10am–noon, 2–6pm Fri–Wed • Free*

Left & Centre **Jardin d'Albertas, Bouc-Bel-Air** Right **Jardins du Château, Ansouis**

TOP 10 Gardens of Provence

1 Domaine du Rayol, Rayol-Canadel-sur-Mer

On one of the most magnificent sites on the coast, Rayol offers a 20-ha (50-acre) overview of Mediterranean-style plant life. Gathered around a pergola and long stairway, a mosaic of eight gardens recreates landscapes of areas of the world with Mediterranean climates. ◈ *Ave des Belges • Map F5 • Open mid-Jan–Nov: 9:30am–12:30pm, 2:30–6:30pm daily • Adm*

2 Jardin de la Villa Ephrussi de Rothschild, St-Jean-Cap-Ferrat

Baroness Rothschild's mansion is legendary *(see p93)*, and its gardens of similar sumptuousness. Seven themed areas (Spanish, Florentine, Japanese and more) are rich with exotic plants, sculptures and fountains *(see p99)*.

3 Jardin d'Albertas, Bouc-Bel-Air

These terraced gardens were laid out in the 1750s and remain a majestic mix of French and Italian influences – ordered in the geometrical style of France, but enhanced by fountains and statuary favoured by Italy. The effect is romantic harmony. ◈ *RN 8 • Map D4 • Open Jun–Aug: 3–7pm daily; May, Sep & Oct: 2–6pm Sat–Sun; rest of year: by appt • Adm*

4 Chartreuse de Bonpas, Caumont

The ruins of a fortified monastery provide a superb setting for two terraces. The first is a formal arrangement of yew and box-trees, shaded by Aleppo pines. The second features a lovely fountain and cascade. ◈ *Map B3 • Open 9am–noon, 2–6pm Mon–Sat • Adm*

Jardins du Château, Ansouis

5 Serre de la Madone, Menton

Anglo-American Lawrence Johnston was a leader among expats who left their mark on Riviera gardens in the early 20th century. His hillside spread is so well landscaped, it barely seems structured at all. Terraces harbour enclosed spaces dedicated to themes or particular exotic plants, and there are fountains water-gardens and a

For Top 10 fragrant Provençal sights **See pp54–5**

collection of statues. ☜ 74 rte de Val de Gorbio • Map H4 • Open 2:30pm Fri for guided tours only • Adm

6 Jardins du Château, Ansouis

The French like to complement their great buildings with formal gardens and this is a fine example. The superb medieval chateau, remodelled during the Renaissance, is flanked by a complex play of terraces. Each is laid out with sculpted box-trees, overseen by firs and pines. ☜ Rue Cartel • Map C3 • Open 2–6pm daily • Adm

7 Val Rahmeh, Menton

More than 700 tropical plants crowd these terraces, established in 1905 by Lord Radcliff, the former governor of Malta. Val Rahmeh specializes in spices, wildflowers, medicinal plants and rare varieties of tomato and potato. ☜ Ave St Jacques • Map H4 • Open May–Sep: 10am–12:30pm, 3–6pm; Oct–Apr: 2–5pm daily • Adm

8 Jardin Exotique, Monaco

A marvellous collection of cactuses, succulents and other semi-desert plants – 6,000 varieties in all. Criss-crossed by a winding path, it is said to be the largest such rockery in the world (see p99).

Jardin Exotique, Monaco

9 Parc Olbius Riquier, Hyères

This 7-ha (17-acre) park contains a dense, varied collection of trees: canary pines, ginkgo biloba, agave and a great selection of palms. There's a little zoo and, in the glasshouse, tropical plants and exotic birds. ☜ Ave Ambroise Thomas • Map E6 • Open 7:30am–5pm daily • Free • DA

10 Jardin Botanique des Cordeliers, Digne-les-Bains

In the centre of town, the garden has a medieval look, planted in squares for the growing of aromatic plants for essences and medicines. More than 350 species recall the importance of plants in Provençal life. ☜ Collège Maria Borély, pl des Cordeliers • Map E2 • Open Apr–May & Sep–Oct: 9am–noon, 2–6pm; Jul–Aug: 9am–noon, 3–7pm daily • Free • DA

For Top 10 Riviera gardens See p99

Left **Café posing** Right **La Colombe d'Or, St-Paul-de-Vence**

🔟 Places to See and Be Seen

1 La Brasserie Carlton, Cannes

La Brasserie's spacious terrace in front of the Carlton Inter-Continental, one of Cannes' exorbitantly luxurious seafront hotels, overlooks the Croisette and is the top place to see and be seen in town, with a magnificent view of the bay. For effect, drink Bollinger *(see p102)*.

2 Planet Hollywood, Cannes

Launched by action heroes Sly Stallone, Bruce Willis and Arnold Schwarzenegger, Planet Hollywood is part of a worldwide chain of movie-themed bar-restaurants and is affordable fun, with potential star-spotting thrown in *(see p101)*.

3 Le Petit Majestic, Cannes

This late night hangout attracts the stay-up-late crowd until the early hours all summer long and the cream of the world's movie business wind up the night here during the film festival *(see p58)*. ❧ *6 rue Allard* • *Map G4*

4 Majestic Hotel, Cannes

One of the flashiest café-terraces attracts some of the world's brightest stars – Roman Polanski, Jude Law and Gabriel Byrne have been sighted – during the film festival and a high-spending, fashionable clientele year-round. Anything stronger than coffee costs a fortune *(see p102)*.

5 Hotel du Cap Eden Roc, Antibes

Book years ahead to mingle with the rich and famous at this luxurious hotel – the flagship of Riviera hedonism. The list of celebrity guests stretches back decades and includes such current stars as Gwyneth Paltrow and Leonardo Di Caprio *(see p140)*.

La Palme d'Or, Cannes

For more luxury hotels **See pp140–41**

6 La Colombe d'Or, St-Paul-de-Vence

This celebrity hideaway hotel and restaurant attracts fashionable artists and celebrities and has a fine private collection of paintings by 20th-century artists including Miró, Matisse and Picasso. By Riviera standards, it is also surprisingly affordable – an overnight stay here need cost no more than an evening drink in one of the flashier clubs in Cannes or Monaco *(see p50).*

7 Les Caves du Roy, St-Tropez

To mingle with the rich, famous and beautiful, book a room at St-Trop's most fashionable hotel and swan into Les Caves du Roy, the hotel's nightclub. Les Caves in season is the haunt of super-models, film stars and racing drivers. Gucci, Versace or Armani almost compulsory *(see p84).*

8 Le Rhul, Marseille

The most prestigious and expensive *bouillabaisse* restaurant in newly fashionable Marseille attracts France's movers and shakers from the worlds of business, media and politics – indeed President Jacques Chirac's dinner bills here became part of a scandal over the perks of French high political office in 2001. ⊗ *296b Corniche JF Kennedy • Map C5 • 04 91 52 54 54 • €€€€*

9 La Palme d'Or, Cannes

The restaurant at the Hotel Martinez is where stars dine, as the signed photos in

Les Caves du Roy, St-Tropez

the foyer attest. The menu is suitably opulent, with lobster and foie gras. Dress to kill and prepare to reach your credit card limit *(see p103).*

10 Le Moulin de Mougins, Cannes

Book a year ahead and you just might get a table at the place where film and three Michelin stars meet at festival time. The rest of the year the waiting list is not as long, but booking is essential. ⊗ *Quartier Notre Dame de Vie • Map G4 • 04 93 75 78 24 • €€€€€*

Left **Le Moulin, Lourmarin** Right **Louis XV, Monte Carlo**

🔟 Gourmet Restaurants

1 Louis XV, Monte Carlo

The world's most glamorous diners expect splendour, and get it amid wood-panelling, gilt mirrors and glistening chandeliers. Splendour on the plates, too, where France's leading chef, Alain Ducasse, works Provençale cuisine into a sensual art form. If you have to think about the expense, you're in the wrong place. ⊗ Pl du Casino • Map H4 • 03 77 92 16 30 01 • €€€€€

2 Les Santons, Moustiers-Ste-Marie

The terrace overlooks the stream rushing through the village; in the dining room, antique Moustiers crockery competes for space with 19th-century paintings. Outside or in, the food refines the best of Provençale cooking. Dishes include fresh pasta with foie gras and truffles or lamb from Sisteron with herbs (see p115).

3 Le Chantecler, Nice

Within the palatial Negresco hotel (see p140), Le Chantecler boasts Regency decor and wood-panelling. The taste is exquisite, as is young chef Alain Llorca's imaginative food, such as green bean salad with light cream, topped with caviar and warm foie gras with mango sorbet (see p91).

4 Le Moulin, Lourmarin

Young chef Edouard Loubet already has a huge reputation for Provençale cooking of great finesse. The surroundings are equally fine, opposite Lourmarin chateau (see p125).

5 La Colombe d'Or, St-Paul-de-Vence

La Colombe welcomed Picasso, Matisse and Braque, among others, who left works instead of payment, so a priceless collection hangs in the restaurant. The place continues to attract celebrities with first-rate Provençale cuisine (see p48). ⊗ Pl de Gaulle • Map G4 • 04 93 32 80 02 • €€€€€

6 Clos de la Violette, Aix

Noted for its skilful use of flavours. Red mullet roasted with smoked bacon is one of the simpler dishes eaten in the dining room or, in summer, in the shaded garden (see p75).

Les Santons, Moustiers-Ste-Marie

Bastide St Antoine, Grasse

7 La Mirande, Avignon
La Mirande was a cardinal's mansion during the popes' time in Avignon. Subsequently it became a sober 18th-century town house, renovated in the 1980s. The restaurant offers fresh, inventive cooking of the highest class *(see p125)*.

8 La Palme d'Or, Cannes
The restaurant of the Hotel Martinez affords magnificent views of the Cannes promenade. This is where the film-making classes go for the best food in town, including Provençale specialities like lambs' feet croquettes with artichoke *(see p103)*.

9 Bastide St Antoine, Grasse
The restored 18th-century country house is superbly sited amid lavender and olive trees above Grasse. Equally splendid is the cooking of chef Jacques Chibois *(see p109)*.

10 L'Oustau de Baumanière, Les-Baux-de-Provence
The converted farmstead dates from the 14th century; the food mixes the rusticity of fresh vegetables and other local produce with top-class cuisine. Ⓢ *CD 27* • *Map B4* • *04 90 54 33 07* • *€€€€€*

Top 10 Regional Specialities

1 Bouillabaisse
Marseille fish dish of up to six species, such as monkfish and John Dory. Spicy stock is served first as soup.

2 Salade Niçoise
Purists use only raw vegetables, hard-boiled eggs, anchovies and olive oil. Others add and tuna.

3 Olives
Signature Provençal product. Introduced by the Greeks in the 4th century BC, olive oil is central to regional dishes.

4 Aïoli
Garlic mayonnaise made with olive oil. Accompanies raw vegetables, cold cod and hard-boiled eggs.

5 Pistou
Thick soup of white, red and kidney beans, pasta and other vegetables, flavoured with basil, garlic and olive oil.

6 Pieds et paquets
Lamb's feet *(pieds)* and stuffed sheep's stomach *(paquets)* in white wine.

7 Ratatouille
Stew of red peppers, courgettes (zucchini), aubergines (eggplant), tomatoes and onions, sautéed in olive oil.

8 Truffles
Hunting of the highly flavoured underground fungus runs mid-November to mid-March. Carpentras is the centre *(see p119)*.

9 Daube
Beef (or wild boar) marinated and simmered in red wine, herbs and garlic.

10 Tapenade
Purée of olives, capers and anchovies, spread on toast. *Anchoïade* is similar, but without capers.

Provence's Top 10

For a guide to restaurant price ranges **See p69**

51

Left **Henri de Saint-Victor, owner of Château de Pibarnon** Right **Grenache vines, Provence**

🔟 Vineyards and Distilleries

1 Château Ste-Roseline
The chateau's Côtes-de-Provence wines have improved tremendously in recent times. Its Cuvée Prieuré has the class to age for 15 years or more, which makes it more than worthy of its historic surroundings. The superb chateau and grounds host summer concerts. ❧ *Sauteraine, Les-Arcs-sur-Argens • Map F4*

2 Château de Berne
British-owned Berne is the region's best wine visitors' centre. The site is picturesque, the welcome friendly and professional and there's a full calendar of cultural events. There's also a first-class hotel-restaurant on-site, L'Auberge. The best wine is the Cuvée Spéciale. ❧ *Chemin Berne, Lorgues • Map F4*

3 Château Romanin
If the stunning underground winery resembles a cathedral, it's not coincidental. The site has had spiritual associations since the Greeks worshipped here in the 4th century BC. The owners aim to harmonize with this past, even programming cultivation by the phases of the moon. The wines, however, are anything but eccentric. ❧ *Romanin, St-Rémy-de-Provence • Map B3*

4 Domaine Rabiéga
In a wooded residential suburb, this Swedish-run domain has a fanatical and innovative attitude to wine quality. The Cuvée Clos d'Ière is among the most expressive of Provençal wines. The welcome at the cellar is both easy and relaxed. ❧ *Clos d'Ière, Chemin Cros d'Aimar, Draguignan • Map F4*

5 Distilleries & Domaines de Provence
Home of Henri Bardouin, the connoisseur's *pastis*. Like all *pastis*, Bardouin is based on star anise but here they add 50 other herbs and spices, many from the surrounding hillsides. The result is an apéritif more richly flavoured than better-known brands. ❧ *Ave St Promasse, Forcalquier • Map D3*

Château de Pibarnon

Domaine de la Citadelle

6 Yves Rousset-Rouard was a film producer and a politician before plunging his fortune into this stylish set-up. The Côtes-de-Luberon wines are treated with respect and the on-site Corkscrew Museum is unique. ✆ *Route de Cavaillon, Ménerbes • Map C3*

Domaine de Beaurenard

7 The Coulon family have been established in Provence's most famous wine village since 1695 – time enough to perfect their skills. The Boisrenard red is the proof. They also run the Musée du Vigneron, the region's best wine museum. ✆ *Rte de Sorgues, Châteauneuf-du-Pape • Map B3*

Domaine St André de Figuière

8 In a superb location, set back from the sea and next to a bird sanctuary, Alain Combard and his family make wines of great finesse. The visitors' entrance to the cellar is, oddly, round the back of a steel tank. ✆ *Quartier St Honoré, La Londe-les-Maures • Map E5*

Domaine de l'Aumérade

9 The quintessential Provence wine domain: the wines, especially the rosés, show true Provençal character. The visit also takes in a museum dedicated to the region's traditional *santon* figurines (see p134). ✆ *Pierrefeu-du-Var • Map E5*

Château de Pibarnon

10 Perched directly above the sea, this may be the most attractively sited wine chateau in Provence. Owner Henri de Saint-Victor has wrestled the unyielding land to produce red wines in the forefront of the Bandol appellation. ✆ *Chemin Croix de Signaux, La Cadière-d'Azur • Map D5*

Top 10 Regional Wines

Châteauneuf-du-Pape
1 At their best, the reds are dark and powerful, the (rarer) whites intensely fruity.

Bandol
2 The home of the mourvèdre grape produces fine and vigorous reds.

Beaumes de Venise
3 France's richest fortified dessert wine, made from the muscat grape.

Côtes-de-Provence
4 Famed for rosés, but now also producing classy reds and heady whites.

Gigondas
5 Sometimes known as "son of Châteauneuf-du-Pape" but the full-bodied wines definitely stand out on their own.

Côteaux d'Aix-en-Provence
6 Fast improving red and rosé wines.

Cassis
7 Fresh, dry whites – particularly good served with Provençale fish dishes.

Côtes du Ventoux
8 The reds, especially, can be very rewarding – although rosés are great for summer picnics.

Côtes du Luberon
9 Another hugely improved group of wines, not least due to investment from fashionable outsiders.

Côtes-du-Rhône Villages
10 In theory, one step up from ordinary Côtes-du-Rhône, but they can be several steps up in practice – especially if the name of the village (such as Cairanne) is mentioned on the label.

Left **Perfume distillation, Grasse** Right **Valensole Plateau**

Fragrant Provençal Sights

1 Sault
When the lavender flowers in July and August, the valley below the little town presents one of the loveliest landscapes in France. It's a tapestry of blue and purple, together with yellow broom, golden cereals and white rock. The town has an excellent Lavender Garden, with more than 100 varieties. 🖎 *Map C3 • Lavender Garden: Open Jul–Aug: tours 11am, 3pm, 5m; Sep–Jun: by appt, DA, Free*

2 Prieuré de Salagon, Mane
The 12th-century Roman-esque priory is the centrepiece of exceptional gardens which illustrate the history of Provence's relationship with its plant life. They range from the Middle Ages to modern times and include an excellent Garden of Aromatic Scents. Within the former mona-stery, an exhibition tells the aromatic plant story. 🖎 *Le Plan • Map D3 • Open May–Sep: 10am–noon, 2–7pm daily; Oct: 2–6pm daily; Nov–Apr: 2–6pm by appt • Adm • DA*

3 Jardin Botanique des Cordeliers, Digne-les-Bains
A history-based herb garden in the centre of town that again celebrates Provence's age-old love of aromatic plants *(see p47).*

4 Jardin de l'Alchimiste, Eygalières
Two gardens in one. First, the Magical Plant Garden, covering plants prized in Provence for their healing properties. Secondly, the Alchemist's Garden, which uses stones, water and plants to re-create symbols alchemists used in their search for the meaning of life. Set around a Renaissance hotel, the place is wonderfully, done. 🖎 *Mas de la Brune • Map D4 • Open mid-May–mid-Oct: 10am–1pm, 3–6:30pm daily • Adm • DA*

5 Musée International de la Parfumerie, Grasse
Many of Provence's aromatic plants are used in the perfume industry. This museum covers perfume's 3,000-year history, from both practical and fashion angles. It includes exhibits from the Chanel fashion house and other designer names, plus Marie-Antoinette's travelling kit and a greenhouse of exotic and regional plants. Perfumes are also available for sale *(see p106).*

Lavender bouquets

6 Valensole Plateau

The second lavender-growing expanse of Provence after Sault also bursts into colour in July and August. Waves of blue and purple roll away towards the Alps. Flanking the road from Riez to Digne-les-Bains, the landscape fills all the senses. ◈ *Map C3*

7 Thermes, Digne-les-Bains

Digne is called "les Bains" (baths) because you can take the waters there. Alongside its medical treatments, however, the modernized thermal establishment also provides an aromatic plant treatment – Jacuzzi with essential oils followed by a massage with more oils. Superbly relaxing. ◈ *Etablissement Thermal de Digne-les-Bains • Map E2 • Open 7am–1pm, 3–6pm daily • Adm*

8 Domaines and Distilleries de Provence, Forcalquier

Producers of herb-based liqueurs, including a *pastis* made with more than 50 plants (see p53).

9 Musée de la Lavande, Le Coustellet

Small but fascinating, the museum covers the story of lavender from field to distillery and beyond. The exhibition of copper stills dates back to the 16th century and there's a video show to explain distillation. ◈ *Rte de Gordes • Map B4 • Open Mar–Dec: 10am–noon, 2–6pm daily • Adm • DA*

10 La Ferme Gerbaud, Lourmarin

The farmstead specializes in herbs, aromatic plants and plants used for dyes. Discover the entire process, from field to finished product. ◈ *Campagne Gerbaud • Map C4 • Open Apr–Oct: 5pm tour daily; Nov–Mar: 3pm tour daily • Adm • DA*

Top 10 Aromatic Plant Products

1 Toiletries
Lavender has always been associated with hygiene, and is used for soaps, perfume and shampoo.

2 Honey
Herbs and lavender provide great pickings for bees.

3 Dried Flowers
Clonal selection has been necessary to create lavender plants whose flowers remain blue even after drying.

4 Food Flavouring
In dried or fresh form, herbs are vital ingredients of Provençal cooking (see p51).

5 Essential Oils
Taken internally or applied externally, Provençal plant distillates have been part of the regional healing armoury for centuries. They need a lot of dilution – follow instructions.

6 Liqueurs
Provençal folk make many alcoholic drinks by macerating or distilling plants – not only *pastis* but also *chicouloun*, *origan de Comtat* (marjoram-based) and others.

7 Herbal Tea
Different sorts of herbal tea can relieve stress, aid digestion and improve sleep.

8 Hulled Lavender Flowers
For perfuming your wardrobe, and keeping moths out.

9 Aromatic Sticks
Once lit, depending on the essence used, the sticks will clean the atmosphere, banish odours or, in the case of citronella, keep mosquitoes away.

10 Candles
Herb-perfumed candles have a nice smell to match the soft light.

Left **Sailing** Right **Windsurfers**

🔟 Sporting Activities

1 Walking
From the coastal paths to mountain tracks inland, Provence could have been created for walkers. Strollers may amble around bays or along woodland paths, while serious hikers can take to the National Hiking Trails (Grandes Randonnées or GR) which criss-cross the region.

2 Sailing
Almost all the coastal resorts have well-equipped pleasure ports and cater for both the beginner and the experienced. The islands of Porquerolles and Bendor *(see pp44–5)* have renowned sailing schools.

3 Climbing
For some of France's finest, toughest rock climbing, head for the Buoux cliffs in the Luberon *(see p117)*, the Verdon Gorges, with 933 routes *(see pp10–11)* or

Rock climbing

the creeks between Marseille and Cassis *(see p66)*. Easier conditions can be found in the Dentelles de Montmirail *(see p118)*.

4 Scuba Diving
The richness of marine life, clear waters and a sprinkling of wrecks all draw divers to the Mediterannean coast. The Iles d'Hyères are noted for their sea-scapes and for the underwater "discovery trail" on Port-Cros *(see p45)*. Cavalaire and Marseille remain, however, the best known and best equipped centres.

5 Canoeing
The classic trip is to canoe down the Verdon Gorges – a two-day, turbulent, 24-km (15-mile) trip from Carrejuan Bridge to Lac de Ste-Croix *(see p11)*. Slightly calmer spirits might prefer canoeing La Sorgue, from Fontaine-de-Vaucluse *(see p118)*.

6 Skiing
Skiing is concentrated where Provence and the Alps meet. In the Ubaye valley, Pra-Loup, Le Sauze and Super-Sauze offer international-standard facilities as, in the Allos valley, do La Foux and Seignus. Meanwhile, there's family-standard skiing on Mont Ventoux – notably at Mont Serein.

7 Golf
The finest golfing can be found at the Frégate golf course, St Cyr, where the sea views are sensational *(see p83)*. Other

For beach activities on the Provençal coast **See p83**

courses offering good golf in lovely surroundings include the Golf de l'Esterel at St Raphaël, the Ballesteros-designed Pont-Royal at Mallemort and Golf de Châteaublanc outside Avignon.

8 Mountain Biking
The marked trails, up and down mountains, through vineyards, forests, gorges and creeks, are endlessly inviting. Figanières is a key centre in the Upper Var while the Alpes de Haute-Provence has some 1,500 km (900 miles) of marked tracks.

Windsurfing

9 Windsurfing
Frequent winds make the Var and Bouches-du-Rhône coasts ideal for board folk. As the Mistral whistles across the Camargue, so windsurfers take advantage at Les-Saintes-Maries-de-la-Mer and Port-St-Louis (see p21).

10 Canyon Running
The exhilarating sport of descending torrents and canyons by abseiling, jumping and swimming has taken off big time. Try it in the Roya valley near Saorge or in any of 70 sites in the Ubaye and Verdon valleys. There are easier descents for beginners in the Pennafort and Destel gorges.

Top 10 Walks

1 Vallée des Merveilles, Mercantour National Park
Serious hikers only on this marvellous mountain trek. Allow 2–3 days, overnighting in refuges. Contact Park HQ before setting out (see p105).

2 Martel Trail, Verdon Gorges
A 15-km (9-mile) trail from Le Palud to Point Sublime. Allow 7–8 hours (see p11).

3 Calanques, Marseille
Spectacular walking along headland trails (see p66).

4 Massif des Maures
The forests, valleys and peaks are criss-crossed with excellent trails (see p83).

5 Coastal Path, Six-Fours-les-Plages
The seaside walk to La Seyne starts off flat, then climbs to the Cap Sicié. Great views. Allow 7 hours. ⊗ Map D5

6 Baou de St-Jeannet, St-Jeannet
The "baou" is the rock overlooking the village near Vence. Stiff but rewarding walk (3–4 hours). ⊗ Map G4

7 Port-Cros, Iles d'Hyères
A paradise of forests, creeks and headlands. Walk the coast in 5 hours (see p44).

8 Dentelles de Montmirail
Trek from Sablet village up to St Amand, the highest point. Six hours (see p118).

9 Vieux Nice
From the Old Town up to Castle Hill and down again: the best in-town walking in the region (see pp16–17).

10 Massif de l'Esterel
The best mountain path is from Pont de l'Esterel to Mont Vinaigre. Four hours (see p78).

Left & Right **Avignon Festival**

Festivals and Events

1 Avignon Festival
France's greatest theatre event is really two festivals. The official one takes over the Papal Palace's Courtyard of Honour *(see p8)* and other venues for modern and classical drama. But it is the unofficial "off" festival which enlivens the town, with street performers and up to 400 shows a day, from dance to burlesque comedy. ⦿ *Jul • Map B3*

2 Nice Jazz Festival
The best of the region's many jazz festivals puts on 75 concerts over eight days. World-famous names, such as BB King and Gil Scott-Heron, show up to play in the 2,000-year-old Cimiez amphitheatre. ⦿ *Jul • Map Q3*

3 Cannes Film Festival
Some 30,000 film professionals attend the world's main cine-gathering, to do business

Gérard Depardieu, Cannes Film Festival

and, incidentally, see a few movies. The atmosphere is glamorously electric. But, as a member of the public, don't expect to meet stars, or even see them, except as they mount the stairs of the Festival Palace for a screening. ⦿ *May • Map G4*

4 Aix Festival
This great lyrical art event has opened up in recent years. As well as classical opera in the courtyard of the Archbishop's Palace, there are more contemporary works, such as Bartók and Britten, recitals and concerts by younger musicians, as well as music masterclasses and street theatre. ⦿ *Jul • Map C4*

5 Musique en Pays de Fayence
Celebrated string quartets bring their music to the lovely Gothic, Baroque and Romanesque churches of the perched villages around Fayence. In a little-known but moving festival, the old stone buildings echo to the works of great masters. ⦿ *Late Oct/early Nov • Map F4*

6 Chorégies d'Orange
France's oldest music festival, started in 1860, has the town's magnificent Roman theatre as its main venue *(see p117)*. The original stage wall ensures perfect acoustics for the classical operas which have earned the event an international reputation. ⦿ *Jun • Map B2*

7 International Piano Festival, Roque d'Anthéron

Since 1980, the festival has drawn the cream of the world's classical and jazz pianists to play beneath the plane trees and night sky at the Château de Florans. ◈ Mid-Jul–mid-Aug • Map F4

8 Nice Carnival

Over three weeks in February, France's fifth city blows all its gaskets as multicoloured floats, grotesque carnival figures and performing troupes take to the streets. Europe's liveliest carnival also features the famous battle of the flowers. ◈ Feb • Map H4

Nice Carnival

9 Fête de la Véraison, Châteauneuf-du-Pape

To celebrate the ripening of their grapes, villagers dress up in medieval guise for street parades and performances and a torch-lit banquet. ◈ 1st weekend Aug • Map B3

10 Fête de la Transhumance, St Rémy-de-Provence

Upwards of 3,000 sheep cram into the old village, for an old-style sheep drive (transhumance) to upland summer pastures. Along with sheep, goats and donkeys are shepherds in traditional costume, food displays and feasting. ◈ May • Map B3

Top 10 Sporting Events

1 Monaco Grand Prix

The jet-set come together for the only street race on the Formula One calendar. ◈ May • Map H3

2 Nikaïa, Nice

This international athletics event is one of the world's Top 10 annual meets. ◈ Jul • Map H4

3 Pétanque World Championships, Marseille

Four days of boules, culminating in a final on the Vieux Port. ◈ Jul • Map K4

4 Olympic Sailing Week, Hyères

Some 1,000 boats from 50 nations compete in this sailing event. ◈ Apr • Map F6

5 Feria du Riz, Arles

Bullfighting and festivities to welcome the Camargue rice harvest. ◈ Sep • Map B4

6 Beach Volleyball World Series, Marseille

The French leg of the World Volleyball Grand Slam, and the richest. ◈ Jul • Map C5

7 Monte Carlo Tennis Masters

One of the tennis circuit's more prestigious events. ◈ Apr • Map H3

8 Olympique de Marseille

The favourite French soccer team (see p66) plays home games July to May.

9 Joûtes Provencales, St Mandier-sur-Mer

Waterborne jousting. ◈ Jul–Aug • Map G4

10 Marathon des Gorges du Verdon

Long-distance running through this dramatic scenery ◈ Sep • Map E3

Left **Château d'If** Right **Pénitents des Mées**

Provençal Legends

1 Saintes-Maries-de-la-Mer
After being set adrift in a boat from Palestine, Mary Jacoby (sister of the Virgin), Mary Salome, Mary Magdalene, Lazarus and servant girl, Sara landed on the Provençal coast. They were the first Christians in Gaul. The "relics" of Jacoby and Salome are found in the town's church, as are those of Sara, patron saint of gypsies *(see p74)*.

2 Man in the Iron Mask
Who was the Man in the Iron Mask? Louis XIV's troublesome brother? A meddling royal priest? No one knows. Certainly, he was dangerous enough to be clamped in the mask and locked away in Château d'If from 1687. You may visit the island fort and see his cell *(see p69).* Map G4

3 Vallée des Merveilles, Mercantour National Park
Almost 4,000 years ago Ligurian tribespeople covered rocks in the Alpine valley with engravings – theories abound about their meaning. The site is superb but difficult to access *(see p105)*.

4 Les Pénitents des Mées
In AD 800 a congregation of monks ogled female Saracen prisoners being led to the River Durance and were turned to stone as punishment. There they remain – a 2-km (1-mile) line of rocks, some 100 m (300 ft) high, looking like repentant monks with their cowls up *(see p114)*.

5 Pont d'Avignon
In 1177 a shepherd boy named Bénézet received orders from God that a bridge should be built across the Rhône. Avignon people were sceptical, so the lad picked up a rock which 30 strong men couldn't shift and carried it to where Pont St-Bénézet was to begin *(see p122)*.

6 La Tarasque, Tarascon
Tarasque, a dragon-like beast, terrorized Tarascon in the 1st century AD, until St Martha sprinkled it with Holy Water. Tarascon converted to Christianity *(see p73)* and Tarasque remains central to the town's June festival.

7 St Maximin-de-la-Ste-Baume
After landing in Provence, Mary Magdalene spread the Christian word, before spending her last

Tarascon

St Maximin-de-la-Ste-Baume basilica

years praying in a cave in the Ste-Baume mountains. Her remains were discovered in the 13th century and may be seen in the Gothic basilica *(see p78)*.

8 Lost "City of God"
The Latin inscription on a rock near St-Geniez indicates the site of a 5th-century "Theopolis", or City of God Christian centre. The rock aside, no trace has been found. However, phenomena including strange lights and odd weather add to the mystery of the place. ⊗ *Map G3*

9 Roussillon
The red cliffs of Roussillon are not coloured by accident. In medieval times the local lord's wife, Sirmonde, fell in love with a troubadour. The lord had him killed and Sirmonde threw herself off a cliff, staining the rocks with her blood *(see p123)*.

10 Cathérine Ségurane, Nice
Washerwoman Cathérine led Niçois resistance against the Turkish fleet that besieged the city in 1543. She knocked out the Turkish standard-bearer with her washboard, before lifting her skirts and putting the rest of the Turks to flight. The day was eventually lost, but Cathérine's statue is in Vieux Nice *(see pp16–17)*.

Top 10 Traditions

1 Midnight Mass, Christmas Eve
Pastoral memories mix with Christian ritual, as live lambs participate in the ceremony.

2 Thirteen Christmas Desserts
Symbolizing Christ and the Apostles, the climax of the Christmas Eve meal includes dried fruit and griddle cakes.

3 Nativity Scene
Scenes mix biblical characters with *santon* figures of Provençal villagers *(see p134)*.

4 Fête de St-Jean
In Valréas medieval parades attend the election of a boy-child to "protect" the town. ⊗ *Map G4 • 23 Jun*

5 Fête des Tripettes, Barjols
Incongruously, celebrates both the relics of St Marcel and the importance of bulls. ⊗ *Map E5 • Mid-Jan*

6 Fête de la Tarasque, Tarascon
Tarasque "reappears" to terrify revellers. ⊗ *Map B3 • last weekend Jun*

7 Fête de la Transhumance, Riez
Sheep cross the village to upland pasture, giving rise to festivities. ⊗ *Map E3 • end Jun*

8 Fête de la Lavande, Sault
The heartland of lavender *(see p54)* celebrates its traditions. ⊗ *Map D3 • 15 Aug*

9 Fête des Mimosas, Bormes-les-Mimosas
Festivities amid the flowers *(see p78)*. ⊗ *Map E5 • 3rd weekend Feb*

10 Fête des Vins, Bandol
The wine district welcomes the new vintage. ⊗ *Map D5 • 1st Sun, Dec*

AROUND PROVENCE

PROVENCE'S TOP 10

Left **Fort St Nicholas** Right **Marseille harbour**

Marseille

THE OLDEST CITY IN FRANCE *was founded 2,600 years ago by Greek
settlers from Asia Minor, and it has barely seen a quiet moment since.
Open-hearted and tumultuous, it is backed by chalk hills and flanked by white
cliffs, with its face to the sea. The sea is Marseille's raison d'être, making it a
trading hub and point of entry for immigrants. As a result, Marseille is a
collection of urban villages, from the souk-like market areas to tiny fishing
settlements. But all the inhabitants are Marseillais: loud, rebellious and volatile.
This is the home of French music, football and bouillabaisse, the most flavoursome fish dish in the world. Picaresque and picturesque, it's a place
in which to feel alive – but keep an eye on your wallet.*

🔟 Sights

1. Vieux Port
2. Notre-Dame-de-la-Garde
3. Le Panier and Vieille Charité
4. Palais Longchamp
5. Musée Grobet-Labadié
6. Les Calanques
7. Prado Beaches
8. Fort St Nicholas
9. Château d'If
10. Musée de la Faïence

1 Vieux Port

Commercial sea traffic might have moved round the corner to newer docks in the 19th century, but the old port remains the heart of city life. Bobbing with pleasure boats and fringed with restaurants, it's where the *Marseillais* gather for festivities and to buy fish at the market. The occupying Germans attempted to subdue the city by blowing up the port's north side in 1943, but Marseille's indomitable nature won the day. ◎ *Map K4*

Notre-Dame-de-la-Garde

2 Notre-Dame-de-la-Garde

This Romanesque-Byzantine church is the symbol of Marseille. Perched on the city's highest hill and topped by a great, gold statue of the Virgin, it can be seen from everywhere in the city and is itself all-seeing: the views from the church are spectacular. Built in the 1850s, the vaulted crypt is carved out of the rock while the sanctuary is rich with mosaics and marble. ◎ *Rue Forte du Sanctuaire • Map K6 • Open 7am–6:30pm daily • Free • DA*

3 Le Panier and Vieille Charité

Wriggling up the hill to the north of the Vieux Port, Le Panier is Marseille's oldest sector. This is where the Greeks settled and, in

Palais Longchamp

subsequent centuries, where the city's immigrants began their new lives. They still do – the tiny streets are alive with different accents and cultures. The main feature is La Vieille Charité, the 17th-century workhouse now transformed into a wonderful cultural centre. It houses the museums of Mediterranean Archaeology and of African, Oceanic and Amerindian Art. Especially noteworthy is the domed central chapel – Italian Baroque at its purest. ◎ *Map J3 • La Vieille Charité: rue de la Charité, Open 10am–5pm Tue–Sun, Adm, DA*

4 Palais Longchamp

Longchamp is the greatest expression of Marseille's 19th-century "golden age". Rich on colonial trade, the *Marseillais* embellished what is essentially just a water tower in palatial Second Empire style. Fountains, columns and animal sculptures evoke abundance and fertility. The central gallery is flanked by two ornate wings, home to the Fine Arts and Natural History museums. Behind the building stretch lush gardens. ◎ *142 blvd Longchamp • Map M3 • Museums: Open 10am–5pm Tue–Sun; Adm*

Carte Privilèges *give one- to three-day access to museums and public transport at substantial savings. Contact the tourist office (see p130).*

Around Provence – Marseille

Les Calanques

5 Musée Grobet-Labadié

Sited opposite the Palais Longchamp, this museum is set in the former private mansion of a 19th-century rich, art-loving Marseille family. Its original decor has been carefully retained, recreating bourgeois life at the peak of the city's prosperity. If the house itself is elegant and sober, the art collection is wonderfully eclectic. Walls are decorated with a unique collection of Gobelin and Aubusson tapestries, while the 10 different salons boast an overwhelming abundance of sculpture, paintings, drawings and furniture from the 13th to 19th centuries, and much more besides. A discreetly sensual delight. ◈ 140 blvd Longchamp • Map M3 • Open 10am–5pm Tue–Sun • Adm • DA (partial)

The Football Capital

First champions of Europe, then enmeshed in match-fixing scandals, the recent history of the Olympique de Marseille football team has matched the turbulence of its home town. But this has done nothing to dissuade the fans of the most popular French team – soccer is the life blood of Marseille life, the Stade Vélodrome its place of worship.

6 Les Calanques

Within 15 minutes of Marseille's centre, you are out of the city and into a different world. Here white rocks plunge into the blue sea and the road snakes into creeks (calanques) of great beauty, and small settlements. This is where the Marseillais spend their weekends, eating, drinking and keeping rich developers out. After the "village" of Les Goudes, the road peters out and access to other, even more picturesque creeks (towards Cassis) is by foot or boat (see p42). ◈ Map C5

7 Prado Beaches

Around the corniche from the Vieux Port and past the tiny, picturesque fishing port of Vallon des Auffes stretch Marseille's resolutely modern beaches. They were reclaimed from the sea with earth excavated during the construction of the city's metro system. Now they run round to the start of the calanques. On summer days, they throb with every conceivable beach sporting activity; at night, the Escale Borély beach area offers some of the town's trendiest nightspots (see p69). ◈ Map C5

8 Fort St Nicholas

On the south side of the Vieux Port is Marseille's fort, built in 1680 by Louis XIV to impose authority on the truculent city – its cannons pointed inland. Star-shaped and built on two levels in pink-tinged limestone, it stares across at the much older St Jean fort. Now split in two by the 19th-century port-side boulevard St Nicholas remains one of the city's most imposing buildings. ◈ Blvd Charles Livron • Map J5

9 Château d'If

This offshore island fortress was built in the 16th century to protect the city's port and was turned into a prison in 1580. Among its inmates were the real Comte de Mirabeau, and the fictional Count of Monte Cristo, the antihero of Alexander Dumas' novel of the same name *(see p37)*. The fortress is accessible by ferry from the Vieux Port. ⊛ *Map C5 • Open May–Sep: daily; Oct–Apr: Tue–Sun • Adm*

10 Musée de la Faïence

The 19th-century Château Pastre is a marvel in itself – set in grounds between sea and hills, its lovely brick and stone façade expresses Marseille's Second Empire stature. The interior decor is equally sumptuous and, since 1995, the chateau has been the setting for a fabulous assembly of pottery, ceramics and earthenware. The collection, from across France and the rest of Europe, numbers nearly 1,500 pieces, from the Neolithic period to the present day. If you previously had any doubts, here's proof that Marseille culture goes deeper than just football. ⊛ *157 ave de Montredon • Map L5 • Open 10am–5pm Tue–Sun • Adm • DA*

Château d'If

A morning exploring Marseille

From the Quai des Belges on the **Vieux Port** *(see p65)* walk up La Canebière, the commercial hub of the 19th-century city where you can still sense the Second Empire grandeur – almost immediately on the left, the Palais de la Bourse (Stock Exchange) is a monumental expression of trading confidence; it now contains the Musée de la Marine detailing Marseille's sea-going history *(Open Tue–Sun • Adm)*. A little further on, at No. 11, is the Musée de la Mode, one of France's best fashion museums *(Open Tue–Sun • Adm)*. At the Neo-Gothic Eglise des Réformés, cross to the place Stalingrad and enjoy a drink by the fountain at Brasserie Danaïdes.

Take the leafy cours Joseph Thierry, then blvd Longchamp to the **Musée Grobet-Labadié** and **Palais Longchamp** *(see p65)*, then wander the lush Longchamp park to place Maréchal Foch. Take the blvd de la Libération, left into rue St Savournin to cours Julien, a lively centre for musicians and artists.

Wriggle down to the place du Marché des Capucins, heart of the city's *souk* market area, then up the style with the designer shops of rue St Ferréol. Place de la Préfecture and rue Edmond Rostand have further galleries, antiques shops and bric-à-brac stalls.

End your morning stroll at place Thiars, a hive of galleries, restaurants and bars. You will have more than deserved your lunch at **Le Caribou** *(see p69)*.

Left **Terres d'Epices** Right **Four des Navettes**

🔟 Specialist Shops

1 Georges Bataille
Finest grocery-cum-delicatessen in Marseille, with irresistible selections of cheese, cold meats, spices, wines and much else besides. ◈ *18 rue Fontange • Map L4*

2 Rue de la Tour
Not one shop but the tiny street where some of Marseille's leading fashion creators congregate, among them Manon Martin, Zenane and Casablanca. ◈ *Map K4*

3 Faïencerie Figuères
Extraordinary enamelled terracotta figures of fruit, vegetables and meat. Artisan works which literally look good enough to eat. ◈ *10–12 ave Lauzier • Map C5*

4 Terre d'Epices
Great, cave-like emporium boasting food from every corner of the globe, from spices of the Indies to Marmite spread. ◈ *43 pl Jean-Jaurès • Map M4*

5 Madame Zaza of Marseille
Now known well beyond Marseille, Zaza's ethnic-style clothes are celebrated for their creativity and playfulness. ◈ *73 cours Julien • Map L4*

6 Souleiado
If you want something Provençal to take home, in the way of fabrics, tableware, linen or clothes, here is a good place to start. ◈ *117 rue Paradis • Map K5*

7 Nouvelles Galeries
The largest store in town is the one-stop shop (clothes, gifts, wines, groceries and more) for those with less time to spare. ◈ *Centre Bourse • Map K3*

8 La Part des Anges
Not only a good wine shop and delicatessen but also a restaurant and sophisticated take-away outlet. In addition, it's open every night until 2am. ◈ *33 rue Sainte • Map J5*

9 La Four des Navettes
The oldest bakery in town and, since 1781, home of the traditional Marseillais *navette*, a small biscuit (cookie) flavoured with orange blossom and, aptly for this port city, shaped like a boat. ◈ *136 rue Sainte • Map J5*

🔟 Dromel Aîné
Even older than the above, Dromel Aîné has been in the business of selling fantastic chocolates, sweets, and a range of unusual teas and coffees since 1760. An unmissable Marseille experience. ◈ *6 rue de Rome • Map L5*

For shopping tips **See p134**

Price Categories

For a three-course meal for one with half a bottle of wine (or equivalent meal), taxes and extra charges.

€	under €30
€€	€30–40
€€€	€40–50
€€€€	€50–60
€€€€€	over €60

Above **Chez Madie**

🔟 Places to Eat

1 Le Miramar
A Marseille institution, serving the finest *bouillabaisse* in town. The views over the Vieux Port from the terrace are splendid. ◊ *12 quai du Port • Map J4 • 04 91 91 10 40 • Closed Sun, Mon • DA • €€€€*

2 Chez Madie
Exceptional Provençale dishes such as *pieds et paquets* and *daube (see p51)*. Excellent value, with Provençal painters exhibited inside. ◊ *138 quai du Port • Map J4 • 04 91 90 40 87 • Closed Sun • DA • €*

3 Café Parisien
Original early 20th-century decor in a restaurant-bar open from 4am to 10pm. Marseille movers and shakers show up for regional fare. ◊ *1 pl Sadi Carnot • Map K3 • 04 91 90 05 77 • €*

4 Les Arcenaulx
Extraordinary vaulted setting in the former 17th-century arsenal. Besides the gastronomic regional restaurant, there is a bookshop, a boutique and an air of mystery. ◊ *25 cours d'Estienne d'Orves • Map K5 • 04 91 59 80 30 • Closed Sun • €€€*

5 L'Escale
Out in the *calanque* of Les Goudes, and with a sea-view from paradise, this restaurant serves up some of the region's best fish. ◊ *4 blvd A. Delabre, Les Goudes • Map C5 • 04 91 73 16 78 • Closed Mon • No credit cards • €€€*

6 Bar de la Marine
Fans of the writer Marcel Pagnol *(see p37)* will recognize the bar's setting from his books. Lunch only. ◊ *15 quai Rive-Neuve • Map K5 • 04 91 54 95 42 • €*

7 L'Epuisette
Set amid Marseille's traditional seaside cabins, L'Epuisette has its feet in the water but its mind firmly on fresh fish. ◊ *Vallon des Auffes • Map C5 • 04 91 52 17 82 • €€€*

8 Escale Borély
Not one establishment, but a collection of beach bars and restaurants with a stunning setting. ◊ *Ave Pierre Mendes-France • Map C5 • €–€€*

9 Les Trois Forts
Great views over the port to accompany fine regional cuisine. ◊ *Hôtel Sofitel, 36 blvd Charles-Livon • Map C5 • 04 91 15 59 56 • DA • €€€€*

10 Le Caribou
First-rate fish and game has been served here since 1945. ◊ *Place Thiars • Map K5 • 04 91 33 22 63 • Closed Sun–Mon, Jun–Sep • DA • €€*

Left **Bouches-du-Rhône landscape** Right **Barbentane château, near Tarascon**

Bouches-du-Rhône

THE BOUCHES-DU-RHÔNE REGION IS WELL NAMED *(bouches means mouths)*, for here the broad channel of France's most important river splits into several separate streams, flowing into the Mediterranean via lagoons and grassy plains. This is the Camargue, a unique wetland now partly protected by conservation areas. The Rhône is Provence's western boundary and for centuries the river was the region's highway. Hence, some of its most important towns grew up along its banks, while villages and medieval abbeys are tucked away in the hills. On the coast, windswept beaches fringe the Camargue, but east of the delta the landscape becomes rocky, with many small coves (calanques).

10 Sights

1. Roman Arles
2. Aix-en-Provence
3. The Camargue
4. St-Rémy-de-Provence and Glanum
5. Les-Baux-de-Provence
6. Abbaye de Montmajour
7. Abbaye de Silvacane
8. Cassis
9. Château du Tarascon
10. Cathédrale d'Images

Cours Mirabeau, Aix

1 Roman Arles
The delightful town of Arles, founded by the Romans, stands on the east bank of the Rhône and is the gateway to Provence from the west (see pp12–13).

2 Aix-en-Provence
Aix is just a stone's throw from the sprawl of Marseille, but keeps its own identity, with cosmopolitan cafés, a grand cathedral and beautiful 18th-century fountains (see pp14–15).

3 The Camargue
This vast expanse of salt marshes, lagoons and grazing land, home to rare bird and animals species, is protected within the Parc National de Camargue and other conservation areas (see pp20–21).

4 St Rémy-de-Provence and Glanum
Overlooked by Les Alpilles, a thickly wooded, miniature sierra of limestone hills, St-Rémy is a perfect exploring base. Mansions built during the 15th and 16th centuries grace its historic centre. One of them was the original home of the de Sade family, ancestors of the notorious Marquis, and now houses a small museum of Roman artifacts, which were found at Glanum, about 30 minutes' walk from the town centre. Here, the site of one of the oldest Greek-Roman settlements in Provence is

Herbs, St-Rémy-de-Provence

landmarked by a magnificent triumphal arch and mausoleum, known collectively as Les Antiques (see p30). ✪ Map B3 • Hôtel de Sade: 1 rue du Parage, St-Rémy; Open Apr–Sep: 10am– noon, 2–6pm daily (until 5pm Oct–Mar); Adm

5 Les-Baux-de-Provence
Perched on a limestone crag, Les Baux is among the most dramatic fortified villages in Provence. A ruined citadel, the Château des Baux, crowns the village. Its walls date from the 10th century AD, when the first Lords of Baux settled here, but the looming Tour du Brau, which guards the entrance and now houses an interesting small museum, is a 14th-century addition. The village is closed to cars (see p38). ✪ Map B4 • Château des Baux: Open 9am–sunset daily; Adm

Les-Baux-de-Provence

Left **Abbaye de Silvacane** Right **Market, Aix-en-Provence**

6 Abbaye de Montmajour

This massive, fortress-like abbey, built by Benedictine monks in the 10th century, can be seen from a great distance. When it was built, the low hill on which it now stands was an island surrounded by pools and marshes and is still, appropriately, known as Mount Ararat. Damaged by fire in 1726, the abbey was restored during the 19th century, and its Eglise Notre-Dame is one of the largest Romanesque buildings in Provence. Below the church, a 12th-century crypt and chapel have been carved into the hillside (see p32). ◎ Rte de Fontvieille, Arles • Map B4 • Open Apr–Sep: 9am–7pm daily; Oct–Mar: 9am–7pm Wed–Mon • Adm

7 Abbaye de Silvacane

Silvacane, along with Sénanque (see pp24–5) and Thoronet, is one of the three great sister-abbeys constructed in the 12th century by the Cistercian order as it rose to prominence in Provence. Its plain, austere architecture

Black Bulls and White Horses

The wild black *taureaux* (bulls) of the Camargue are one of the symbols of Bouches-du-Rhône, along with the sturdy white horses – direct descendants of the prehistoric wild horse of Europe. These are still ridden by the *gardians*, the sombrero-wearing cowboys of the Camargue pastures.

reflects the rule of the order, which was founded by St Bernard in protest at the luxury and corruption of other monasteries. The church has a high, vaulted transept and the cloister arcades and refectory were added in the 13th and 14th centuries. Abandoned by its monks in the late 14th century, it became a living abbey once again in the 20th century. ◎ La Roque d'Anthéron • Map C4 • Open Apr–Sep: 9am–7pm daily, Oct: 10am–1pm, 2–5pm, Wed–Mon • Adm

8 Cassis

This delightfully pretty fishing port (see p39) with its brightly coloured fishing boats anchored in a harbour on a rugged, rocky coastline, was a favourite with painters such as Dufy, Derain and Matisse (see pp36–7), all of whom were inspired by its clear light and bright Mediterranean hues. Amazingly, it has escaped being spoiled by tourism, and there are pretty rocky coves (calanques) and beaches nearby. Cassis is also noted for its excellent seafood (fresh sea urchins are considered a local delicacy) and there are plenty of good restaurants. ◎ Map D5

9 Château de Tarascon

The white battlements of the Château de Tarascon seem straight from a historical romance. Built to guard a vital crossing of the Rhône on Provence's borders, the riverside castle has steep, crenellated curtain walls between massive round towers and looks impregnable. Begun by King Louis of Anjou, ruler of Provence in the 15th century, it was completed by his successor, King René. On his death, Provence became part of France (see p29) and the castle lost its strategic importance, becoming a prison until 1926 (see p60). ◈ Blvd du Roi René, Tarascon • Map B3 • Open Apr–Sep: 9am–7pm, Oct–Mar: 9am–noon, 2–5pm daily • Adm

10 Cathédrale d'Images

Opposite Les Baux, and with a great view of the village, is the dramatic Val d'Enfer, where the soft rock of the cliffs has been eroded by wind and water into weird twisted shapes. Old cuttings show where the easily worked rock was quarried to build the houses and battlements of the village. One of these quarry tunnels has now been turned into a remarkable spectacle, with thousands of beautiful Renaissance frescoes projected on to the 20-m (65-ft) high walls of the artificial cavern. ◈ Rte du Val d'Enfer • Map B4 • Open Mar–Sep: 10am–7pm; Oct–Feb: 10am–6pm daily • Adm

Château de Tarascon

Little Rome: A Morning in Arles

🕐 Start the day with a visit to the largest and most striking Roman monument in Provence, **Les Arènes** (see p12). From the highest tier of seats you have a fine view of the historic centre and the Rhône. From here, walk across to the **Théâtre Antique** (see p12), for another glimpse of Roman Arles, then walk down the rue du Cloître to the place de la République, where water gushes from bronze masks at the foot of an obelisk, brought here from Egypt by the Romans.

On the east side of the square, visit the fine Romanesque **Eglise St-Trophime** (see p12), with its lovely sculpted pillars crowned by little figures of saints and martyrs. Follow the rue de l'Hôtel de Ville to **Les Thermes de Constantin** (see p12), the remains of a palace built for a 4th-century AD Roman emperor. Then spend up to an hour in the Musée Réattu (rue du Grand-Prieuré • open daily • adm), with its fine collection of 18th–20th-century art, including works by Picasso.

Another great painter, Van Gogh, is associated with place du Forum, cluttered with cafés – one has been painted to look just as it was in his work Café la Nuit (see p75). Stop in for ☕ coffee. End the morning at the Museon Arlaten (rue de la République • open Tue–Sun • adm), where the largest folklore collection in Provence recalls the region's rich and fading traditions (see pp60–61).

Left **Ceiling, Abbaye de St-Michel de Frigolet** Right **Doll's carriage, Château de Barbentane**

Best of the Rest

1 Centre de Ginès and Parc Ornithologique du Pont-de-Gau, Camargue

For a spectacular view of the Camargue, visit the information centre and bird park, where enclosures display the lagoons' bird life *(see p20)*. ◈ Map B5 • Open 10am–sunset daily • Adm

2 Musée Camarguais, The Camargue

The Camargue comes to life in this fascinating museum, housed in a farmhouse *(see p20)*. ◈ Mas du Pont de Rousty • Map B5 • Open Apr–Sep: 9:15am–5:45pm daily; Oct–Mar: 10:15am–4:45pm Wed–Mon • Adm

3 Château de Barbentane

This delightful Italianate mansion was built in 1674 and is ornately decorated with 17th-century antiques. ◈ Map B3 • Open Mar–Oct: 9am–noon, 2–5.30pm Thu–Tue (daily Jul–Sep); Nov–Mar: 9am–noon, 2–5.30 pm Sun • Adm

4 Notre-Dame des Saintes-Maries-de-la-Mer

Dominating the seaside village, this 12th-century church *(see p32)* houses relics of St Sarah and has superb views from its roof terrace. ◈ Pl de l'Eglise • Map B5 • Open 8am–6pm daily • Adm to roof

5 Eygalières

This village was the source of Arles's water supply in Roman times, via an aqueduct. A 12th-century church and ruined castle stand in the village. ◈ Map B4

6 Château de l'Emperi, Salon-de-Provence

The imposing chateau was once the seat of the archbishops of Arles. It now houses a collection of military uniforms. ◈ Montée du Puech • Map B4 • Open 10am–noon, 2–6pm Wed–Mon • Adm

7 Abbaye de St-Michel de Frigolet

The most attractive aspect of this 19th-century abbey is its brightly painted depictions of saints. ◈ Map B3 • Open 9am–noon, 2–7pm Wed–Mon • Adm

8 Château de Beaucaire

Facing the Château de Tarascon *(see p73)* is this ruined 11th-century chateau. For part of the year it hosts falconry displays. ◈ Pl Raymond VII • Map B3 • Open Mar–Nov from 2pm daily • Adm

9 Abbaye de St-Roman

This remarkable 5th-century abbey is one of the oldest in France, and the only troglodyte monastery in Europe. ◈ Map B3 • Open Apr–Sep: 9am–7pm daily; Oct: 10am–1pm, 2–5pm Wed–Mon • Free

10 Musée Baroncelli, Saintes-Maries-de-la-Mer

This museum celebrates Marquis Folco de Baroncelli-Javon (1869–1943), who spent his life maintaining the traditions of Camargue *gardians (see p72)*. ◈ Rue Victor Hugo • Map B5 • Open 10am–noon, 2–6pm Wed–Mon (until 5pm Sep & Mar) • Adm

Price Categories

For a three-course meal for one with half a bottle of wine (or equivalent meal), taxes and extra charges.

€	under €30
€€	€30–40
€€€	€40–50
€€€€	€50–60
€€€€€	over €60

Above **Pavement café, Aix-en-Provence**

Places to Eat

1 Le Clos de la Violette, Aix-en-Provence

Superb restaurant in which chef Jean-Marc Banzo uses the best Provençal ingredients to create memorable dishes *(see p50)*. ◎ *10 ave Violette • Map C4 • 04 42 23 30 71 • No vegetarian options • €€€€€*

2 L'Olivier, Arles

Dishes unique to the region, such as Camarguais bull steaks, served in a pretty courtyard. ◎ *1 bis rue Réattu • Map B4 • 04 90 49 64 88 • No vegetarian options • €€€*

3 Lou Marques, Arles

Dishes such as gigot of lamb and risotto of *coquilles St-Jacques* (scallops) served in the restaurant of this four-star hotel. There is also a terrace. ◎ *Hôtel Jules César, 9 blvd des Lices • Map B4 • 04 90 52 52 52 • No vegetarian options • €€€€*

4 Le Café la Nuit, Arles

Painted yellow to look like the café in Van Gogh's painting *(see p35)*. Food is run-of-the-mill but good value, and the location on the square is ideal. ◎ *11 pl du Forum • Map B4 • 04 96 44 56 • No credit cards • No vegetarian options • DA • €*

5 Marc et Mireille, Beauduc

This restaurant is on a remote stretch of beach reached by rough roads – but its fresh fish make it worth the journey. ◎ *Map B5 • 04 42 48 80 08 • No credit cards • No vegetarian options • €€*

6 Le Relais Ste-Victoire, Beaureceuil

Seasonal produce served in cosmopolitan ways, such as eggs poached in cream of truffles, are the key note here. ◎ *Map B4 • 04 42 66 94 98 • Closed Sun–Mon, Jan–Feb • No vegetarian options • DA • €€€*

7 L'Amphytrion, Aix-en-Provence

Noted equally for its wine list as its menu, which features favourites such as Sisteron lamb in a tapenade crust. Pretty terrace too. ◎ *2 rue Paul Doumer • Map C4 • 04 42 26 54 10 • Closed Sun–Mon • No vegetarian options • DA • €€*

8 La Camargue, Aigues-Mortes

This restaurant serves fish and steak in a summer garden, or in front of a fire in winter, with live gypsy music. ◎ *19 rue de la République • Map A4 • 04 6 53 86 88 • Closed Mon • No vegetarian options • DA • €*

9 La Regalido, Fontvieille

Gastronomic restaurant using local seafood and Provençal ingredients, such as garlic and herbs. ◎ *Rue Mistral • Map B4 • 04 90 54 60 22 • Closed Mon, Tue L, Sat L • No vegetarian options • €€€€€*

10 Vitamine, Arles

One of the few vegetarian havens in the region, with 50 different salads and pasta dishes. ◎ *16 rue du Dr Fanton • Map B4 • 04 90 93 77 36 • Closed Sun • €*

Left **Massif de l'Esterel** Centre **Cathedral, Fréjus** Right **Bas-relief, Basilica St-Maximin**

The Var and Provençal Coast

WITHIN A 30-MINUTE DRIVE OF THE GLAMOUR of St-Tropez, you can be on a rugged mountainside so remote that you dread nightfall. That's the charm of the Var – an intoxicating mix of the easy life and a harsh landscape. In the Verdon gorges and Upper Var, nature is both wild and imposing; down below, beauty assumes more rounded forms in beach resorts and casinos. Yet the Provençal tendency to "let time take its time" unites the region. Little wonder that this is the most popular of French holiday regions.

🔟 Sights

1. Abbaye du Thoronet, Le Thoronet
2. Sanary-sur-Mer Harbour
3. Fréjus Old Town
4. Massif d'Esterel
5. Port Grimaud
6. Place des Lices, St-Tropez
7. Basilica St-Maximim, St-Maximim-la-St-Baume
8. Bormes-les-Mimosas
9. The Caves, Villecroze
10. Musée des Arts et des Traditions Populaires, Draguinan

St-Tropez old town

1 Abbaye du Thoronet, Le Thoronet

There is much manmade splendour in Provence, but little to touch the majesty of this 12th-century Cistercian abbey, built in a wooded dip near Lorgues. Probably the finest example of Romanesque architecture in the region, along with its sister houses, Silvacane and Sénanque (see pp24–5), it rises with sober magnificence. The un-mortared stones of the church, monks' buildings and cloisters are decorated only by changing sunlight, their interior volumes inspiring awe and serenity. The harmony of structure and setting make contemplation unavoidable. ◎ *Quai Abbaye • Map E4 • Open Apr–Sep: 9am–7pm; Oct–Mar: 10am–1pm, 2–5pm • Adm*

2 Sanary-sur-Mer Harbour

The prettiest harbour in the Var remains a proper fishing port, bobbing with boats. Beyond, palm trees fringe a frontage of pastel façades which dance in the sunlight. Activity varies from relaxed to intense, notably during the morning market which enlivens the Allées d'Estienne-d'Orves. The beach is nearby. So, too, are plaques commemorating Thomas Mann, Bertolt Brecht and other German writers who took refuge from the Nazis here in the 1930s. ◎ *Map D5*

Abbaye du Thoronet

3 Fréjus Old Town

Despite its relaxed beach-bag and flip-flop image, the town of Fréjus has an exceptional double heritage. As Forum Julii, it was the second port of the Roman Empire in the region and retains some of the oldest and most extensive ancient remains in Provence. Particularly notable are the elliptical, 12,000-seater arena and theatre (see p30). Meanwhile, the town's medieval bishopric status has left it with an extraordinary group of episcopal buildings. The 12th-century cathedral incorporates a wonderful octagonal baptistry from an earlier, 5th-century church while the 14th-century cloisters have ceilings painted with bracingly lurid events from the Apocalypse (see p32). Definitely not to be missed out from any tour of the Var region. ◎ *Map F5 • Episcopal Group: pl Formigé, Open 9am–noon, 2:30–6:30pm Tue–Sun, Adm*

Harbour, Sanary-sur-Mer

Cloisters, Basilica St-Maximin

4 Massif de l'Esterel

As the rugged red rocks of the Esterel range plunge into the blue of the Mediterranean, they create creeks and contrasts of stirring beauty. Inland, the tough, volcanic mountains may rise no higher than 600 m (2,000 ft) but the landscape is of breathtaking gorges, passes and peaks. Many paths and tracks provide access to the mountainscape and its rich tree life. Take the Perthus or tougher Mal-Infernet valleys – in the footsteps of brigands who hid out here *(see p57)*. ◈ *Map G4*

5 Port Grimaud

Built in the mid-1960s over former marshland, the port is reminiscent of Venice, as brightly painted houses push out onto quays separated by canals but joined by little bridges. Access is by boat or by foot. Although now weathered and wearing a real Provençal look, traditionalists still prefer medieval Grimaud, perched 5 km (3 miles) inland. ◈ *Map F5*

6 Place des Lices, St-Tropez

Generations of artists, stars and beautiful people have made this village square possibly the best known in the world. But it remains just that – the rich and famous may come and go, but the Tuesday and Saturday markets are always here *(see p18)*. ◈ *Map F5*

7 Basilica St-Maximin, St-Maximin-la-Ste-Baume

The finest example of Gothic architecture in Provence was erected to house the relics of Mary Magdalene, "discovered" on the site in 1280. The basilica appears unfinished from the outside (there is no belfry) but within, the sense of space and balance is stunning. So too are the treasures, notably a 16th-century altarpiece depicting the Passion and a renowned 17th-century organ. Mary Magdalene's remains are in a reliquary and a marble sarcophagus in the crypt. ◈ *Map D4 • Open 9am–6pm daily • Free*

Perched Villages

The Var's *villages perchés* were built as a defence against Saracen pirates. In the 9th century Saracens occupied parts of the Var, notably around La Garde Freinet. Expelled in 973, they returned to wreak havoc at frequent intervals up until the 18th century. The locals therefore took to the hills as a form of protection.

Port Grimaud

Troglodyte dwellings, Villecroze

8 Bormes-les-Mimosas
A glorious village, unravelling down its hillside in a cascade of little streets, stairways and flowers (see p38). ❀ Map E5

9 The Caves, Villecroze
Riddling the wall of rock which dominates the medieval village, these caves were first home to prehistoric folk and, later, provided refuge against marauding Saracens. Most startling, however, is a cave on the north side of the village, transformed by a 16th-century nobleman into a four-storey, fortified house. The Renaissance frontage, staircases and windows cut out of the stone can still be seen. A spring within the caves creates a cascade which waters gardens below. ❀ Map E4 • Guided tours May–Jun: 2–6pm; Jul–mid-Sep: 10am–noon; 2.30–7pm daily; mid-Sep–mid-Oct: 2–6pm Sat–Sun • Adm

10 Musée d'Arts et Traditions de Moyenne Provence, Draguignan
Housed in 18th-century buildings in the heart of the old town, this is one of the best ethnographic museums in France. It tells the story of Provençal life from its earliest days to the beginning of the 20th century with tableaux, models, reconstructions and audio-visual devices. ❀ 15 rue Roumanille • Map F4 • Open 9am–noon, 2–6pm Tue–Sat, 2–6pm Sun • Adm

---

A Day's Drive on the Massif des Maures

Morning

🕐 Start in the village of Grimaud and take the D558 up to **La Garde Freinet** (see p82). Continue 7 km (4 miles) before turning left (D75) towards Gonfaron and stop at the Village des Tortues where the rare native Hermann tortoise can be seen (quartier Plaine • Open Mar–Nov: 9am–7pm daily • Adm). Take the D39 towards **Collobrières** (see p82). At Col des Fourches head up to Notre-Dame-des-Anges, the Maures's highest point. There's a fascinating chapel and outstanding views.

Three km (2 miles) before Collobrières, turn left (D14) to the Chartreuse de la Verne, a 12th-century Carthusian monastery of local serpentine stone (quartier Verne • Open 11am–5pm daily • Adm). Then double back to Collobrières. Stop for a drink or lunch at **La Petite Fontaine** (see p85).

Afternoon

Leave towards Pierrefeu, but 2 km (1 mile) later turn left (D41) towards **Bormes-les-Mimosas**. The dramatic drive, between wooded slopes and plunging valleys, takes you over the Col de Babao to the N98. Turn left towards La Molo, but stop at the Arboretum de Gratteloup (N98), a forest garden with 50 tree varieties.

Continue to La Mole, then turn right (D27) to the Col du Canadel and stop at the **Domaine du Rayol** gardens (see p46). Returning to Grimaud, reward yourself with dinner at Le Côteau Fleuri (pl des Pénitents • 04 94 43 20 17 • Closed Tue • €€).

Following pages **Pruning vines after the grape harvest**

Left **Ramatuelle** Right **View from Collobrières**

Var Villages

Around Provence – The Var & Provençal Coast

1 Le Castellet
The only access to this glorious perched village is via two gates in its 13th-century walls. Within, steep paved streets climb tortuously to the feudal castle. Views over olive groves to the sea are outstanding. ◈ Map D5

2 Mons
Almost 820 m (2,700 ft) up, Mons has the heritage to match its grandiose position: remains of the great Roche Taillée Roman aqueduct run nearby (see p31). In the village itself, narrow alleys wind around ancient porches, arcades and the wonderful 12th-century church. A gem. ◈ Map F4

3 Collobrières
It's difficult to resist a village claiming to be "world capital of candied chestnuts". In the heart of the Maures mountains (see p79), Collobrières is surrounded by forested slopes. ◈ Map E5

4 Les Arcs-sur-Argens
With the medieval castle up top, the rest of the old village hugs the rocky promontory. Its labyrinth of streets and vaulted stairways unfolds to the modern village below. ◈ Map F4

5 Ramatuelle
Although swamped by the overspill from St-Tropez in summer, Ramatuelle remains a lovely hilltop village. Its tiny streets and vaulted passages are heavy with flowers. ◈ Map F5

6 La Cadière-d'Azur
The medieval St-Jean gate is a great introduction to this ravishing maze of streets set above the terraced hillsides and vineyards of Bandol. The sun is warm, the air scented and the panorama breathtaking. ◈ Map D5

7 Tourtour
Remote, perched 600 m (2,000 ft) up and surrounded by pine forest, this is a picturesque tangle of streams, medieval buildings and old stone streets leading to a main square lined with restaurants. ◈ Map F5

8 Comps-sur-Artuby
This is high, wild country, where the Knights Templar made a base. The 12th-century St-André chapel testifies to their presence, and affords unbeatable views over the nearby Artuby Gorges. ◈ Map F4

9 La Garde-Freinet
Nestling amid forests of cork-oak and chestnut, La Garde-Freinet stands sentry to the wild Maures Mountains. Higher still are the ruins of the medieval village fortified by Saracens. ◈ Map F5

10 Callas
Fortified on the side of a green hill, Callas has a winding, self-contained charm imposed by its isolation near the edge of the Canjuers Plateau. It's also a fine base for walking the nearby Pennafort Gorges. ◈ Map F5

Visit the Var villages off-season and you will find a world before tourism took its hold on the region.

Left **Jet-skiing, Var coast** Right **Windsurfers**

Sporting and Outdoor Activities

1 Watersports
The Var coast offers everything, from sailing and tuna-fishing through to windsurfing and parascending. Resorts awarded the *"Station Voile"* symbol for excellent watersports facilities include Hyères and Bandol *(see p56)*. Meanwhile, Brutal Beach at Six-Fours draws international windsurfers *(see p57)* and Cavalaire claims to be the French capital of jet-skiing.

2 Hill Walks in the Maures Mountains
The walking possibilities amid these forests, valleys and peaks are magnificent. Among the best is the two-hour trek from Collobrières to the Chartreuse de la Verne monastery *(see p79)*.

3 Cycling on Porquerolles
Cars are banned, so cycling is the most rewarding way to discover the island. Hire bikes from the village *(see p42)*.

4 Mountain Biking
Tough trail cyclists are spoiled for choice in the Var. The most dramatic trips are around the Verdon gorges *(see pp10–11)* but Draguignan, Figanières and Fréjus also provide challenging routes.

5 Scuba Marine Park, Port-Cros
An underwater guided path. Hire flippers, snorkel and a mask, make for Le Palud beach and follow the buoys to discover posidonia,

coral, mother-of-pearl and brightly coloured fish. It is vital you call the tourist office before setting out. ✆ *Tourist office: 04 94 01 40 70*

6 Coastal Walk, St-Tropez
Far from the summer crowds, the path winds around creeks and beaches, vines and pines, offering exceptional views. From Graniers beach to Cap Camarat takes six hours.

7 Golf
The Var has a dozen golf courses, of which the best-known is the Golf de Frégate, set among vineyards and olive groves and overlooking the sea. ✆ *Golf de Frégate, rte de Bandol, St Cyr-sur-Mer • Map E5*

8 Formula One Driving
Try the one-day course, open to all drivers at the Le Luc circuit. Expensive but undeniably thrilling. ✆ *AGS Formule 1, Circuit du Var, Gonfaron • Map F5 • 04 94 60 97 00*

9 Mont Faron
Rising 600 m (2,000 ft) behind Toulon, Mont Faron is most dramatically reached by cable car from blvd Admiral Vence. The views and walks are terrific. ✆ *Map E5*

10 Sailing, Lac Ste-Croix
This vast artificial lake *(see p11)* offers all sorts of boating, from pedalo through to dinghy. It's also an access point for canoe trips up the gorges. ✆ *Map F3*

Left and right **La Playa, Fréjus**

TOP 10 Var Nightlife

1 Les Caves du Roy, St-Tropez
The Byblos Hotel's legendary club has a suitably strict door policy: the unfashionable are generally unfortunate. Once selected, you're at the heart of Tropezien nightlife *(see p49)*. ◎ *Ave Paul Signac • Map F5*

2 Le Papagayo, St-Tropez
This pillar of the resort's jet-set nightlife since 1962 shows no signs of fading. Progress from the terrace restaurant via the cocktail bar to the dance floor, to mingle with the trendy, and possibly famous. ◎ *Le Port • Map F5*

3 Casino des Palmiers, Hyères
Renovated in the 1990s, the casino has retained its *belle époque* style, added on a glass dome and widened its horizons. Alongside the gaming rooms are a hotel, restaurant and nightclub. ◎ *Ave Ambroise Thomas • Map E6*

4 La Playa, Fréjus
This hotspot livens up the beachfront with outside dance floors. Thursday evenings offer a buffet dinner then dancing till dawn. ◎ *Blvd Libération • Map F4*

5 Bar à Thym, Toulon
The city's hippest late-night bar offers more than 200 beers, 100 whiskies and music from salsa to trip-hop. The restaurant specializes in fresh fish. ◎ *32 blvd Cunéo, Le Mourillon • Map E5*

6 Le Paradise, Le Lavandou
After more than 60 years of existence Le Paradise remains the centre for night-time groovers. Resembling a circus big-top, it has evolved effortlessly into the techno era. ◎ *Blvd Front de Mer • Map F5*

7 Le Grand Casino, Bandol
A stylish spot in which to play the fruit machines, the tables – or the field – in two different nightclubs, Le Must and Le Blackjack. The complex also boasts a reputable restaurant. ◎ *Pl Lucien Artaud • Map D5*

8 Sun Rock Café, Hyères
The jazz 'n' rock rendezvous is the best nightspot in town. As well as music (both disco and live), it lays on art exhibitions and internet connections. ◎ *20 ave de Belgique • Map E6*

9 Le Bora-Bora, Le Lavandou
A brasserie by day, Le Bora-Bora becomes a buzzing music bar by night. Wash down the Latino-Caribbean rhythms with a fine choice of cocktails. ◎ *Rue Charles Cazes • Map F5*

10 Le Cocotier, Toulon
Given the name (*cocotier* means coconut palm), it's no surprise that this spot specializes in sunshine sounds, whether from stage or turntable. Dress is smart, the atmosphere welcoming. ◎ *330 ave de Claret • Map E5*

Above **L'Arbousier, St-Raphaël**

Price Categories

For a three-course meal for one with half a bottle of wine (or equivalent meal), taxes and extra charges.

€ under €30
€€ €30–40
€€€ €40–50
€€€€ €50–60
€€€€€ over €60

🏆10 Places to Eat

1 Hostellerie Bérard, La Cadière d'Azur

This former monastery offers distinctly non-monastic standards of luxury and innovative Provençale cuisine. ◉ *6 rue Gabriel Péri • Map F5 • 04 94 90 11 43 • Closed Sat L, Mon L, mid-Jan–mid-Feb • €€€€*

2 Mas du Langoustier, Ile de Porquerolles

Between forest and sea at the west end of the island, the Langoustier is the definition of tranquillity and the Mediterranean cooking is worthy of its setting. ◉ *Map E6 • 04 94 58 30 09 • Closed mid-Oct–Apr • DA • €€€€*

3 Hostellerie de l'Abbaye de La Celle, La Celle

Deceptively simple Provençale fare in lovely 18th-century buildings. ◉ *Pl du Général-de-Gaulle • Map F5 • 04 98 05 14 14 • Closed mid-Jan–mid-Feb • DA • €€€€*

4 Les Pins Penchés, Carqueiranne

A few steps from the port. The *pissaladière* of rock mullet is particularly tasty. ◉ *39 ave Général-de-Gaulle • Map F5 • 04 94 58 60 25 • Closed Sun D, Mon, Tue L • DA • €€€*

5 Le Logis du Guetteur, Les Arcs-sur-Argens

This 11th-century castle is now a superb restaurant. In winter, dining is in the lookout tower; in summer on the terrace. ◉ *Pl du Château • Map F4 • 04 94 99 51 10 • Closed Wed, mid-Jan–mid-Feb • €€€*

6 L'Arbousier, St-Raphaël

In the heart of town, serving cooking of startling inventiveness, such as *carpaccio* of prawns in a marjoram vinaigrette. ◉ *6 ave de Valescure • Map F5 • 04 94 95 25 00 • Closed Sun D, Mon, Wed D • €€€*

7 Les Moulins, Ramatuelle

This fine old inn breathes class, as does the gastronomic Provençale cooking. ◉ *Rte des Plages, lieu-dit Les Moulins • Map F5 • 04 94 97 17 22 • Closed Wed, Oct–Mar • DA • €€€€*

8 Auberge de la Mole, La Mole

This welcoming village inn has forged its reputation on classical dishes: pâtés, foie gras and confit de canard. ◉ *RN98 • Map F5 • 04 94 49 57 01 • Closed Mon • No credit cards • DA • €€€*

9 La Bastide des Magnans, Vidauban

La Bastide takes the simplest Provençal ingredients and comes up with a balanced array of wonderful tastes. ◉ *32 ave Maréchal Galliéni • Map F5 • 04 94 99 43 91 • Closed Sun D, Mon, Wed D • DA • €*

10 La Petite Fontaine, Collobrières

Excellent, no-frills regional cooking (*soupe au pistou* or game in season) in a characterful restaurant on the village square. ◉ *Pl de la République • Map E5 • 04 94 48 00 12 • Closed Sun & Mon. L • No credit cards • DA • €*

➲ **Note:** Unless otherwise stated, all restaurants accept credit cards and serve vegetarian meals

Left **Musée Marc Chagall** Right **Promenade des Anglais**

Nice

NICE – THE VERY WORD SPARKLES WITH SUNLIGHT AND GLAMOUR. *In the 19th century, the European aristocracy colonized the place, drawn by the glorious curve of the Bay of Angels and the mild winter weather. More recently, it has been the turn of film stars to endow France's fifth city with a legacy of luxury. And there's a legacy of culture, too. Artists such as Matisse and Chagall were inspired by Nice's limpid light and left their mark here with their abstract works (see pp36–7). Alongside this opulence, however,*

there is another Nice, rooted in Mediterranean history and fiercely independent. The city voted to join France only in 1860 (it had for centuries been part of the kingdom of Savoy) and retains its own Niçois dialect, cuisine and traditions. It is from the marriage of these two different halves that the real fascination of Nice is born.

Mansion, Cimiez Hill

🔟 Sights

1. Vieux Nice
2. Promenade des Anglais
3. Musée Matisse
4. Musée d'Art Moderne et d'Art Contemporain (MAMAC)
5. Musée des Beaux-Arts
6. Cimiez Hill
7. Musée Marc Chagall
8. Port Lympia
9. Parc Floral Phénix and Musée des Art Asiatiques
10. Cathédrale St-Nicolas

Around Provence – Nice

1 Vieux Nice
The city's heart, filled with the aroma and sounds of all things Niçoise (see pp16–17).

2 Promenade des Anglais
The world's best-known seafront boulevard owes its name to the English community which funded its initial construction in 1822. Inspired by Anglican vicar Lewis Way, the community was keen to give work to the local poor. Now flanked by traffic lanes separated by flowerbeds and palms, the "Prom" sweeps majestically round the Bay of Angels. Belle époque edifices, notably the magnificent Hotel Negresco (see p140) recall Nice's days as a magnet for European nobility. The substance has gone, but the style remains. Map N5

3 Musée Matisse
Shortly before his death in 1954, the artist (see p36) donated a collection of paintings to the city in which he had lived for 37 years. They have found a superb home in a 17th-century Italianate villa on Cimiez Hill

Musée d'Art Moderne et d'Art Contemporain

overlooking the city centre. Boosted by subsequent donations, the collection affords a comprehensive overview of Matisse's work, from 1890 through to the gouache cut-outs of his later years. It is made all the more effective by the presentation of items from his daily life (see p34). 164 ave des Arènes de Cimiez • Map Q1 • Open 10am–6pm Wed–Mon (until 5pm Oct–Mar) • Adm

4 Musée d'Art Moderne et d'Art Contemporain (MAMAC)
Conceived as a triumphal arch on four marble columns linked by transparent walkways, the museum's modern architecture is startlingly effective. It is an exceptional setting for collections tracing the story of the avant garde from the 1960s to the present day. Particularly notable are the US Pop Artists and European New Realists, including Nice's own Yves Klein (see p35). Promenade des Arts • Map Q4 • Open 10am–6pm Wed–Mon • Adm

Trompe l'oeil façade, Musée Matisse

5 Musée des Beaux-Arts

The 19th-century townhouse built for a Ukrainian princess with a taste for luxury is a marvel of Neo-Classical excess. Within is one of southern France's best collections of art from the 17th to early 20th centuries. The highlight is on the first floor, which

Musée d'Art Moderne et d'Art Contemporain

provides a panorama of 19th-century French art, through to the Impressionists and Post-Impressionists. On the ground floor are 17th- and 18th-century works, while the patio and garden are adorned by Rodin sculptures. ⊗ *33 ave des Baumettes • Map N5 • Open 10am–noon, 2–6pm Tue–Sun • Adm*

6 Cimiez Hill

When European nobility took to wintering in Nice, they colonized Cimiez Hill with mansions and hotels. The grandiose Boulevard de Cimiez is, thus, sumptuous with gardens and magnificent villas in styles from Louis XV, to Neo-Gothic, to Oriental. Most impressive of all is the Excelsior Regina Palace, a *belle époque* masterpiece where

Queen Victoria once stayed. Most of the edifices now house apartments, but the opulence remains palpable. ⊗ *Map Q2*

7 Musée Marc Chagall

Amid lovely gardens, this museum was purpose-built to house Chagall's 17 great works on the "Biblical Message" *(see p36)*. The collection was later supplemented by oils, sketches, pastels and gouaches, donated by the Russian artist himself. He also created stained-glass windows, a mosaic and tapestry for the museum. The whole provides the world's best opportunity to appreciate Chagall and the spiritual themes which fascinated him *(see p34)*. ⊗ *Ave du Dr Ménard • Map Q3 • Open 10am–6pm Wed–Mon (until 5pm Oct–Jun) • Adm*

8 Port Lympia

Dug in the mid-18th century, the port never took off commercially and remains quieter than most Mediterranean city harbours. It is all the more charming for that, a haven of pleasure boats and cruise-ships, surrounded by splendid Italianate buildings. Little wonder that the visiting Russian playwright Chekhov considered this the most pleasing part of Nice. ⊗ *Map R4*

Nice's Expat Community

Led by the British, European (notably Russian) nobility flocked to Nice in wintertime from the early 19th century. Vast, luxurious hotels, villas and places of entertainment sprung up to accommodate them. Nice became two cities – one for the wealthy and leisured northern visitors and another for working Mediterranean natives. This era disappeared with World War I, but somehow the glamour never left.

---

9 Parc Floral Phénix and Musée des Arts Asiatiques

This large floral park is a themed wonderland of world horticulture with, at its centre, Europe's biggest greenhouse. Inside the metal and glass "marquee", one wanders through recreated warm-climate zones, from equatorial forest to the Natal desert. The park is also the setting for the Asian Arts Museum, a marble and glass construction built over an artificial lake. It contains classical and contemporary creations from the principal Asian civilizations. ✪ *405 Promenade des Anglais • Map N5 • Park: Open 9am–7pm daily (until 5pm mid-Oct–mid-Mar), Adm • Museum: Open 10am–6pm Wed–Mon (until 5pm Oct– Jun), Adm*

10 Cathédrale St-Nicolas

The Russian community was almost as prominent in Nice as the British in the late 19th and early 20th centuries. With the backing of Tsar Nicolas II, this Russian Orthodox cathedral was completed in 1912 as the community's focal point. ✪ *Rue Nicolas II • Map N4 • Open 9am–noon, 2:30–6pm (summer), 9:30am–noon, 2:30–5:30pm (winter) Mon–Sat • Adm*

Cathédrale St-Nicolas

A Morning Walk around Nice

🕐 Start at the Tourist Office (5 Promenade des Anglais), then turn left along avenue de Verdun to place Masséna, the city's central square. Take in the glorious red façades, gardens and ornamental fountains before crossing to enter **Vieux Nice** *(see pp16–17)* on rue Alexander Mari. Turn right into rue de l'Opéra and left into rue St-François-de-Paul, an old-fashioned street with long-established shops, notably Auer for confectionery (No. 7) and Alziari for olive oil (No. 14). Proceed to Cours Saleya for the celebrated flower market, then turn into tiny rue Gaëtan to soak up the old town atmosphere. Before leaving the old town, don't fail to take in the cathedral, the magnificent Palais Lascaris, place St-François fish market and the narrow, shop-filled rue Pairolière.

Emerge into the relative peace and 18th-century harmony of place Garibaldi, then take rue Dr-Ciaudo to the splendid **MAMAC** *(see p87)*, where you can spend an hour or so admiring the museum's wonderful modern art. Back in the fresh air, stroll along Boulevard Carabacel with its elaborate mansions.

At place Magenta, forget culture and start shopping. For designer fashion proceed into rue Paradis then avenue de Suède. Rue de Rivoli then brings you to the legendary **Hotel Negresco** *(see p140)*. If you're feeling rich, lunch in its **Chantecler** restaurant *(see p91)*; if watching the pennies, have a look anyway: its interior abounds in ornate treasures.

Left **Casino Ruhl** Right **Hotel Negresco, home to Negresco Piano Bar**

TOP 10 Nightspots in Nice

1 Casino Ruhl
The original Neo-Classical Ruhl building has sadly gone, to be replaced with a more Las Vegas-style set-up. It offers gaming tables, cabaret, a disco on Friday and Saturday nights and slot machines until dawn. ◈ *1 promenade des Anglais • Map N5*

2 La Civette du Cours
"Bar sympa", they say in French, which means friendly and appealing – especially for the young, artistic and mildly eccentric. ◈ *1 cours Saleya • Map Q5*

3 L'Ambassade
The trendiest spot in town stays that way by operating a selective door policy. Once among the élite, you'll be consumed by the techno atmosphere. ◈ *18 rue du Congrès • Map P5*

4 Wayne's
Home-from-home for English people in this pub in Vieux Nice. Good beer, pub food, live music, table dancing and a terrace. ◈ *15 rue de la Préfecture • Map Q5*

5 Le Klub
Immensely popular club, especially, but not exclusively, for gays. ◈ *6 rue Halévy • Map P5*

6 L'Escalier
The first room is music, either live DJ, rock and jazz, the second is billiards, beer and big screen TV. The whole is convivial. ◈ *10 rue de la Terrasse • Map P5*

7 Negresco Piano Bar
No techno here in the bar of the city's palatial hotel *(see p140)*. Just the tinkling of ivories amid wood panelling and deep armchairs, which give the place the pleasingly languorous air of a gentleman's club. ◈ *37 promenade des Anglais • Map N5*

8 Le Blue Boy
The two bars on two floors provide a stylish, fashionable gathering place for the trendier elements of the gay community. ◈ *9 rue Spinetta • Map P5*

9 L'f
Pronounced "Lef", this is one of the friendliest places for a drink and a bite to eat on the Vieux Nice nighttime circuit. A year-round venue – the terrace is heated in winter. ◈ *6 pl Charles Félix • Map P5*

10 Scarlett O'Hara's
Irish bars are terribly fashionable with the French – and this one is no exception. Live Irish music and a lively atmosphere add to the attraction. ◈ *22 rue Droite • Map P5*

Above **La Merenda**

Price Categories

For a three-course meal for one with half a bottle of wine (or equivalent meal), taxes and extra charges.	€ under €30
	€€ €30–40
	€€€ €40–50
	€€€€ €50–60
	€€€€€ over €60

🔟 Places to Eat

1 Le Chantecler
Palatial setting within the Hotel Negresco for Alain Llorca's renowned Provençale-inspired *haute cuisine (see p50).* 🕭 *27 promenade des Anglais • Map N5 • 04 93 16 64 00 • €€€€€*

2 Le Grand Pavois
Also known as "Chez Michel", in honour of the owner. The decor is a bit out-dated, but the welcome is warm and the regional food is outstanding. Dinner only. 🕭 *11 rue Meyerbeer • Map P5 • 04 93 88 77 42 • €€*

3 La Merenda
Formerly at Le Chantecler, Dominique le Stanc turned his back on superchef stress to open this little restaurant. No telephone, no pretension – just simple excellence. 🕭 *4 rue Terrace • Map P5 • Closed Sat–Sun • No credit cards • €€*

4 L'Acchiarde
Locals sip their apéritifs at the counter and from the kitchen comes simple, flavoursome food (fresh ravioli, *tournedos au gorgonzola*). 🕭 *38 rue Droite • Map R5 • 04 93 85 51 16 • Closed Sat D, Sun, Aug • No credit cards • No vegetarian dishes • €*

5 Don Camillo
A refined setting on the edge of Vieux Nice for the most refined Niçois cooking available. Try the stuffed ravioli *à la Niçoise.* 🕭 *5 rue des Ponchettes • Map R5 • 04 93 85 67 95 • €€€*

6 Le Boccacio
The decor recalls that of a schooner – but it's stylish, rather than kitsch, as befits a restaurant specializing in seafood. 🕭 *7 rue Masséna • Map R5 • 04 93 87 71 76 • €€*

7 Nissa La Bella
A family atmosphere and great Niçoise dishes like vegetables stuffed with minced meat. 🕭 *6 rue Ste-Réparate • Map R5 • 04 93 62 10 20 • Closed Tue & Fri L, Oct • €*

8 Le Comptoir
Fashionable folk eat excellent Niçoise fare in trendy Art Deco surroundings. 🕭 *20 rue St-François-de-Paul • Map R5 • 04 93 92 08 80 • Closed Sat & Sun L • €€*

9 Le Safari
Seafood and meat dishes served on one of the liveliest terraces of Vieux Nice. 🕭 *1 cours Saleya • Map Q5 • 04 93 80 18 44 • €*

10 Nissa Socca
Nissa means Nice, and *socca* is the local chickpea flour pancake, and this is one of the best places to eat it. 🕭 *7 rue Ste-Réparate • Map R5 • 04 93 80 18 35 • €*

Note: Unless otherwise stated, all restaurants accept credit cards and serve vegetarian meals

Left **Prince's Palace** Right **Roquebrune-Cap-Martin rooftops**

Monaco and the Riviera

THE FRENCH RIVIERA, stretching from Cannes to the Italian border, is the most mythologized stretch of Mediterranean coastline. In the 19th century its balmy winter climate attracted plutocrats, princes and their entourages, and its clear sunlight and vivid colours drew a new breed of painters. In the 1920s it became a summer resort for the first time, and in the 1950s and 1960s it was the epitome of jet-set chic and the habitat of film stars, musicians and millionaires. You could say that this is where modern tourism really started. In high summer there seems to be hardly a square metre of beach, a yacht mooring, parking space or café table left vacant, while off-shore or in Antibes' harbour float the cruisers of the mega-rich. This is a coast like no other and all you can do is surrender to its mystique. Meanwhile, the enclave of Monaco, an independent state since the 14th century, has a character all of its own.

🔟 Sights

1. Casino de Monte Carlo
2. Musée Picasso
3. Prince's Palace
4. Villa Ephrussi-Rothschild
5. Château Grimaldi
6. Marineland
7. Musée Renoir
8. Roquebrune-Cap-Martin
9. Sales des Mariages
10. Villa Kerylos

Riviera promenade

1 Casino de Monte Carlo

This monument to *belle époque* splendour is also the heart of the region's famous gambling industry – well worth a look whether you want to play the stakes or simply soak up some glamour *(see pp26–7)*.

Picasso ceramic jug, Musée Picasso

pebble patterns, is a wonderful setting for summer concerts. The Compagnie des Carabiniers du Prince, in full dress uniform, changes the guard daily at 11.55am. ⊗ Pl du Palais • Map H4 • Open Jun–Sep: 9.30am–6.30pm; Oct: 10am–5pm daily • Adm

2 Musée Picasso, Antibes

A bishop's palace during the Dark Ages, this building then fell into the hands of the Grimaldi lords of Monaco, before becoming the seat of the royal governors of the region. Today, it is one of the finest art museums in the world, housing 300 works by Spanish artist Pablo Picasso *(see p36)*, who worked here in 1946 and donated 25 of his drawings and paintings and more than 100 ceramic pieces. Work by other artists, including Léger, Ernst, Modigliani and Miró, is also on exhibition *(see p34)*. ⊗ Château Grimaldi, Vieux Port • Map G4 • Open Oct–May: 10am–noon, 2–6pm Tue–Sun; Jun–Sep: 10am–6pm Tue–Sun • Adm

3 Prince's Palace, Monaco

Built on the site of a 13th-century Genoese fortress, the seat of the Grimaldi princes of Monaco, flanked by centuries-old cannons, is even more imposing inside than out. Not to be missed are the superb frescoes of mythological scenes by 16th-century Genoese artists, the opulent blue-and-gold Louis XV Salon, the finely crafted woodwork of the Mazarin Salon and the gorgeous Throne Room. The main courtyard, the Cour d'Honneur, with its geometrical

4 Villa Ephrussi de Rothschild, St-Jean-Cap-Ferrat

The most palatial of all the villas built in the Riviera's plutocratic heyday was the dream of Beatrice Ephrussi de Rothschild (1864–1934), a daughter of the wealthy banking family. Its lavish Neo-Classical façade conceals an opulent interior of arcades surrounded by a covered courtyard hung with magnificent tapestries. Superb antiques and sketches by Fragonard also feature, while the gardens are as sumptuous as the interior *(see p46)*. ⊗ 1 ave Ephrussi de Rothschild • Map G4 • Open 15 Feb–Oct: 10am–6pm daily; Jul–Aug: 10am–7pm daily; Nov–14 Feb: 2–6pm Mon–Fri • Adm • DA to ground floor only

Villa Ephrussi-Rothschild

The Grimaldis of Monaco

Monaco's Grimaldi dynasty is the oldest ruling family in the world. François Grimaldi, disguised as a monk, seized the castle in 1297. By 1489 France and Savoy recognized Monaco's independence. In 1612 Honore II was the first lord to take the title of prince. During the French Revolution the prince and his family were ousted, to be restored to their throne in 1814.

5 Château Grimaldi, Haut-de-Cagnes

Built as a Grimaldi fortress in 1309, this castle's battlements dominate the landscape of Haut-de-Cagnes. Inside the walls, however, is a wonderful surprise: a sumptuous palace, built in 1620 by Jean Henri Grimaldi. Today it houses a clutch of museums and art collections including a museum of modern Mediterranean art, a museum dedicated to the olive tree, and a collection of portraits of the renowned 1930s *chanteuse*, Suzy Solidor. ◈ *9 pl Grimaldi • Map G4 • Open May–Sep: 10am–noon, 2–6pm; Oct–Apr: 10am–noon, 2–5pm Wed–Mon • Adm*

Renoir's studio, Musée Renoir

6 Marineland, Antibes

Killer whales, playful dolphins and fearsome sharks are all inhabitants of Marineland, on the outskirts of Antibes. The theme park also has a farm and petting zoo, a butterfly and reptile jungle, and the largest water park on the Riviera, with 12 giant chutes, a sea-water wave pool, a large swimming pool, as well as three miniature golf courses. ◈ *Rte National 7, Antibes • Map G4 • Open 10am–8pm daily • Adm • DA*

7 Musée Renoir, Cagnes-sur-Mer

The former home of artist Auguste Renoir has been preserved almost exactly as it was on his death in 1919. Ten of his paintings are on display, including *Les Grandes Baigneuses* (1892), along with works by his friends Raoul Dufy and Pierre Bonnard. The house is surrounded by olive groves *(see p35)*. ◈ *19 chemin des Collettes • Map G4 • Open May–Sep: 10.30am–12.30pm, 1.30–6pm; mid-Nov–Apr 10am–noon, 2.30–5pm Wed–Mon • Adm*

Château Grimaldi courtyard

8 Roquebrune-Cap-Martin

The Château de Roquebrune, perched on its hilltop above Cap-Martin, is said to be the oldest feudal castle in France. Built more than 1,000 years ago, it has been remodelled more than once, by the Grimaldi clan and, in the early 20th century, by a wealthy Englishman, Sir William Ingram, who added a mock English tower. Down at sea level, a lovely coastal path leads all the way to Monaco, passing 19th-century villas set in luxurious gardens *(see p39)*. 🖉 *Map H3*
• *Château de Roquebrune: pl du Château, Roquebrune, Open 10am–12:30pm, 2–5pm daily, Adm*

9 Salle des Mariages, Menton

The eclectic genius Jean Cocteau decorated this room in Menton's town hall in 1957, adorning it with colourful pictures of a fishing couple and the tragic story of Orpheus and Eurydice, a legend by which he was fascinated. More of his work can be seen in the Musée Jean Cocteau on the seafront *(see p35)*. 🖉 *Hôtel de Ville, pl Ardoino • Map H3 • Open 8.30am–12:30pm, 1.30–5pm Mon–Fri • Adm*

10 Villa Kerylos, Beaulieu-sur-Mer

Theodore Reinach (1860–1928) conceived this remarkable building, constructed between 1902 and 1908, as a perfect Classical Greek villa, in imitation of the palace of Delos in Greece, dating from the 2nd century BC. Copies of ancient mosaics and frescoes evoke the world of the Greek city states, and the seaside location is striking. 🖉 *Map F4*
• *Open for guided tours only: 2pm, 3pm, 4pm, 5pm Mon–Fri (& 11am Sat–Sun) • Adm • DA*

A Morning Tour of The Rock

Start this walk around the oldest part of Monaco, where the Grimaldis founded their principality. Visit the state apartments and the **Prince's Palace** *(see p93)*, taking in the lavish salons, throne room and 17th-century chapel.

From place du Palais it is a short walk along rue Basse, one of the most picturesque streets in the old quarter, to No. 27, the Wax Museum of the Princes of Monaco *(Open 10am–4pm Tue–Sun • Adm)*. Here tableaux act out episodes from the history of the Grimaldi dynasty. Carry on along rue Basse to the Museum of the Chapel of the Visitation, on place de la Visitation *(Open 10am–4pm Tue–Sun • Adm)*. Housed in the 17th-century Baroque chapel are works by artists Rubens and Zurbaran.

At the end of rue Basse, turn right and double back along avenue St-Martin to the Oceanographical Museum *(Open 10am–6pm daily • Adm)*. You'll need at least 90 minutes here to view the tanks of marine fauna from all over the world. Don't miss the new giant aquarium with its fearsome sharks and majestic stingrays. Enjoy lunch in the museum's restaurant and savour the view of the Riviera and the Esterel hills from its terrace, before rounding off your day with the 30-minute ride on the Azur Express tourist train. This leaves from the museum on a round trip past the port, the palace, casino and ornamental gardens.

Left **Plage d'Agay Beach** Right **Port St-Lucia**

TOP10 Beaches and Watersports

1 Plages de la Croisette
One long beach stretches all the way along the Cannes esplanade, sectioned off into tiny private beaches, with umbrellas, loungers and snack bars with waiter service. Most offer water-skiing. ◎ *Map G4 • Open May–Sep: 8am–sunset daily • Adm*

2 Plage d'Agay
Watersports on this beautiful beach include waterskiing, wind-surfing and parascending, as well as more relaxing boat excursions. ◎ *Map F5*

3 Théoule
The pretty beach at Théoule, surrounded by hills, bustles in summer. Kayaks and pedaloes are available for rental. ◎ *Map G4*

4 Port St-Lucia, St-Raphaël
Try eight different water-sports including parascending, waterskiing and windsurfing, just outside St-Raphaël, with a one-day discovery pass sold at the tourist office. ◎ *Map G5 • Free • DA*

Windsurfers, Côte d'Azur

5 Vieux Port, St Raphaël
St Raphaël is the coast's top dive centre, with shipwrecks from World War II and a range of wall dives off the rocky coast. There are several dive outfits at the Vieux Port – a list is available from the tourist office. ◎ *Map G5*

6 Club Nautique d'Antibes, Antibes
The club offers windsurfing, dinghy and catamaran sailing and yacht charters for all levels, with crewed yachts available by arrangement. ◎ *Map F4 • Open 8am–sunset daily*

7 Plage de la Siesta, Antibes
This beach offers a range of adrenaline sports that includes bungee-jumping, waterskiing and parascending. ◎ *Map F4 • Open May–Sep: 8am–sunset daily • Adm • DA*

8 Plage Helios, Juan-les-Pins
Exciting parascending and, for the even more adventurous, breathtaking flights aboard micro-light float-planes. ◎ *Map F4 • Open May–Sep: 8am–sunset daily • Adm • DA*

9 Marineland
A huge family aquapark with 12 chutes, a wave pool and several swimming pools including one for toddlers *(see p94)*.

10 Palais des Festivals
Perhaps not the most luxurious beach in Cannes, but it is no more crowded than the pay beaches and it's free. ◎ *Map F4*

For the Top 10 best beaches in Provence **See pp42–3**

Above **Jardin Exotique, Monaco**

🔟 Riviera Gardens

1 Villa Ile de France, Musée Ephrussi de Rothschild
Gorgeous formal gardens and lily ponds surround the pink-and-white villa built by Beatrice Ephrussi de Rothschild *(see p93).*

2 Jardin Exotique, Monaco
The largest collection of succulent rock plants in the world. Within the gardens is a 60-m (200-ft) deep cave with spectacular limestone formations. 🖉 *62 blvd du Jardin Exotique • Map H4 • Open mid-May–mid-Sep: 9am–7pm; mid-Sep–mid-May: 9am–6pm or sunset • Adm*

3 Parc Fontvieille and Princess Grace Rose Garden, Monaco
Palm and olive groves and a small lake surround 4,000 roses planted in memory of Princess Grace of Monaco, who died in a car accident. 🖉 *Fontvieille • Map H4 • Open 9am–sunset daily • Free • DA*

4 Japanese Gardens, Monaco
This formal garden is a triumph of Zen horticulture and a striking contrast to the classic gardens of the Riviera. 🖉 *Ave Princesse Grace, Monte Carlo • Map H4 • Open 9am–sunset daily • Free • DA*

5 Casino Gardens, Monaco
Laid out around the casino *(see pp26–7)* these are classic 19th-century gardens, with trim lawns and water features. 🖉 *Pl du Casino, Monte Carlo • Map H4 • Open 9am–sunset daily • Free*

6 Jardin Exotique, Eze
The exotic gardens planted around the clifftop village offer superb views far out over the Mediterranean. 🖉 *Rue du Château • Map H4 • Open 9am–5.30 pm daily • Adm*

7 Jardin Botanique Exotique, Menton
Laid out by English expatriate Lord Radcliffe in 1905, this garden is planted with sub-tropical shrubs. Visits by arrangement with the Maison du Patrimoine. 🖉 *Ave St-Jacques • Map H3 • Maison du Patrimoine: 5 rue Ciapetta, 04 92 10 97 10, Adm*

8 Parc Thuret, Cap d'Antibes
Superb collection of Mediterranean trees and shrubs founded by Gustave Thuret in 1857 in the grounds of his villa. 🖉 *62 blvd du Cap • Map G4 • Open 8.30am–5.30pm daily • Adm • DA*

9 Parc Vaugrenier, Antibes
Many rare plants are among the species to be seen in this park, with its 11 km (7 miles) of walking trails, and freshwater lagoon. 🖉 *Chemin des Groules, RN7 direction Villeneuve Loubet • Map G4 • Open 9am–5.30pm daily • Free • DA*

10 Villa Eilenroc Gardens, Cap d'Antibes
Charles Garnier, designer of the Monte Carlo Casino, built this magnificent villa, set in an 11-ha (27-acre) park with trees from all over the world. 🖉 *Fondation Beaumont, ave de Beaumont • Map G4 • Open 9am–5pm Tue–Wed • Free • DA*

For the Top 10 best gardens in Provence **See pp46–7**

Around Provence – Monaco & the Riviera

Left and right **Designer shops, La Croisette, Cannes**

TOP 10 Places to Shop

1 La Croisette, Cannes
Cannes' esplanade is a great place for shopping or window-shopping, with famous labels such as Chanel (appropriately, at No. 5) Christian Dior (No. 38), Celine (No. 24), Louis Vuitton (No. 44) and Cartier (No. 57). *Map G4*

2 Rue d'Antibes, Cannes
For that absolutely fabulous Cannes look, head straight for the Rue d'Antibes and its string of designer boutiques, all breathtakingly expensive and dazzlingly ostentatious. *Map G4*

3 Avenue des Beaux-Arts and Allée Serge Diaghilev, Monaco
With plenty of cash floating around, Monaco is a magnet for designer shops and *haute couture*. Try these two streets for the latest look. *Map H4*

4 Vallauris
Vallauris's moribund pottery industry was revived when Picasso took an interest in the craft and more than 100 local potters sell their work on its streets in summer. *Map G4*

5 Le Marché Forville, Cannes
This open-air market overflows with flowers, seasonal fruit and vegetables, fresh fish and local products. It's a great place to buy Provençal delicacies to take home. Open daily except Sunday. On Mondays, it becomes a flea market. *Map G4*

6 Galerie du Metropole, Monaco
Get the Monaco look at an affordable price at this shopping centre which houses a selection of designer shops selling *prêt-à-porter* clothes, shoes and accessories. *Map H4*

7 Nouvelles Galeries, Menton
You will find four levels of international designer and brand name clothes and accessories for men, women and children, all under one roof. Free parking, too. *Rue de la République • Map H4*

8 Cours Masséna, Antibes
One of the last authentic covered markets on the Riviera bustles with life every morning until noon and is perfect for buying all sorts of local delicacies to take home. *Map G4*

9 Antiques Market, Antibes
Rummage through stalls selling everything from cut glass and statuary to antique porcelain, lace, embroidery and linen in search of something small enough to carry home. Thursday and Saturdays, from 8am to noon. *Rue Aubernon, blvd Clemenceau and rue de Fontevielle • Map G4*

10 Villeneuve Loubet
Villeneuve Loubet supports a thriving arts scene and is full of artists' and sculptors' studios where you can invest in an original work of art by a living artist. *Map G4*

Left **Casino de Monte Carlo** Right **Jimmy'z**

🔟 Riviera Nightspots

1 Casino de Monte Carlo
The epitome of Riviera glamour, luxury and gambling excess *(see pp26–7).*

2 Planet Hollywood, Cannes
Restaurant, café and disco, owned by film stars, comes into its own during the Film Festival but is a hot spot year round and is easy to get into. ◈ *1 Allées de la Liberté • Map G4 • 04 93 06 78 27 • €€*

3 Carlton Casino Club, Cannes
On the seventh floor of this very smart hotel, formal dress is required to gain access to the exclusive gaming rooms. Celebrate winning with a glass of champagne, or drown your sorrows in a very dry martini – shaken, not stirred, of course. ◈ *Carlton Inter-Continental Cannes, 58 La Croisette • Map G4*

4 Bar des Celebrités, Cannes
Billed as "the place to have a drink in the company of stars", but even during the Film Festival, you are unlikely to rub shoulders with the A list. One of the best bars in Cannes, nonetheless. ◈ *Carlton Inter-Continental Cannes, 58 La Croisette • Map G4*

5 Jimmy'z, Cannes
Proving that the 1970s never really died, this long-standing Cannes nightspot is *so* Riviera. Dress flash to fit in with the crowd of middle-aged groovers who still make this their club of choice. Drinks average a breathtaking €40, however. ◈ *Casino Croisette, Palais des Festivals • Map G4*

6 Le Whisky a Go-Go, Cannes
Blisteringly loud music, a pounding beat and a sweaty atmosphere separate the middle-aged swingers from the real party animals in this popular Cannes disco. ◈ *115 ave des Lérins • Map G4*

7 Le Cesar's Palace, Cannes
This is Cannes imitating Las Vegas, imitating ancient Rome. A cavernous club, with a relaxed door policy and live rap, dance and groove artists at weekends. ◈ *48 blvd de la République • Map G4*

8 Disco 7, Cannes
Loud and louche, Disco 7 attracts a mixed gay and straight crowd. Techno and transvestism make for a decadent atmosphere. Not for the faint-hearted. ◈ *7 rue Rouguière • Map G4*

9 Stars 'N' Bars, Monaco
Currently the most popular disco and restaurant in Monaco, with transatlantic tastes in food, drink and music and a young, wealthy clientele. ◈ *6 quai Antoine 1 • Map H4*

10 Le Blitz, Cannes
Rock and roll on a budget (by Cannes standards) in this disco which also features live bands and has better musical taste than most venues around town. ◈ *22 rue Mace • Map G4*

For a guide to restaurant price ranges **See p103**

Left **Chevre d'Or, Eze** Right **Le Cactus, Eze**

🔟 Cafés with Terraces

1 Café de Paris, Monte Carlo
In front of the casino (see p27), under white umbrellas and baskets of flowers with the Mediterranean in the background, the Café de Paris is a delightful place for an *al fresco* meal or a drink. ◊ Pl du Casino • Map H4

2 Majestic Hotel, Cannes
Sip your drinks slowly on this deeply fashionable hotel terrace which attracts the *crème de la crème* of the film business during the International Film Festival. A glass of bubbly here costs as much as a meal in many other spots. ◊ Map G4

3 La Brasserie Carlton, Cannes
The terrace of the Carlton Inter-Continental is the top place to see and be seen in Cannes, with a superior view of the bay and promenaders along the Croisette. ◊ Carlton Inter-Continental Cannes, 58 La Croisette • Map G4

4 Bar & Boeuf, Monte Carlo
Famed chef Alain Ducasse's terrace restaurant serves only sea bass and beef. After dinner, skip the queue to get into Jimmy'z next door (see p101) via the restaurant's private entrance. ◊ Le Sporting, ave Princesse Grace • Map H4

5 Villa Kerylos, Beaulieu-sur-Mer
The seaside terrace of this replica of an ancient Greek villa, overlooking the Mediterranean

and surrounded by pine-clad hills, is one of the most pleasant places to eat and drink along the coast (see p95).

6 La Villa Piano Bar, Cannes
The terrace of this restaurant-bar, in an attractive 19th-century villa, is shaded by leafy vines and has live music almost every evening in summer. ◊ 7 rue Marceau, Cannes • Map G4

7 Le Relais Martinez, Cannes
The terrace restaurant of this top Cannes hotel wins praise for its excellent menu, with many dishes in common with the Palme d'Or (see p103). ◊ Hotel Martinez, 73 blvd La Croisette • Map G4

8 Chèvre d'Or, Eze
It's worth staying at this gorgeous chateau hotel just to enjoy breakfast on its clifftop terrace, looking out over the sea below (see p143).

9 Hôtel L'Aiglon, Menton
The seafront at Menton is a solid strip of open-air cafés, but this elegant hotel's café-terrace, set back from the main drag, is the most stylish. ◊ 7 ave de la Madone • Map H3

10 Le Cactus, Eze
If your budget won't stretch to the Chèvre d'Or, this modest café has the same stunning views for a fraction of the price and serves delicious *crêpes*. ◊ Rue de la Porte • Map H4

Left **Le Cagnard, Cagnes-sur-Mer**

Price Categories

For a three-course meal for one with half a bottle of wine (or equivalent meal), taxes and extra charges.

€	under €30
€€	€30–40
€€€	€40–50
€€€€	€50–60
€€€€€	over €60

🔟 Places to Eat

1 Zebra Square, Monaco
Nouvelle cuisine in chic, minimal surroundings. Salmon with seven different tartare sauces is one imaginative offering. 🛇 *Grimaldi Forum, ave Princesse Grace • Map H4 • 03 77 99 99 25 50 • DA • €€€*

2 Neat, Cannes
British chef Richard Neat excels with dishes such as snails with morel mushrooms and asparagus shoots. 🛇 *11 sq Mérimée • Map G4 • 04 93 99 29 19 • DA • €€€*

3 La Palme d'Or, Hôtel Martinez, Cannes
A grand address and a menu to match. Dress your best for a meal to remember *(see p51)*. 🛇 *73 blvd de La Croisette • Map G4 • 04 92 98 73 00 • Closed Mon–Tue • DA • €€€€€*

4 Villa des Lys, Hôtel Majestic, Cannes
The imaginative menu includes such dishes as lobster in a shellfish sauce. 🛇 *14 blvd de la Croisette • Map G4 • 04 92 98 77 41 • DA • €€€€*

5 Les Deux Frères, Monaco
Good Provençale food with the emphasis on lamb, duck and seafood. 🛇 *Pl des Deux Frères • Map H4 • 04 93 28 99 00 • Closed Sun • DA • €*

6 La Terrasse, Juan-les-Pins
A garden terrace, a glass roof which opens for summer, and a wonderful seafood menu. 🛇 *Hôtel Juana, La Pinède, ave Galice • Map G4 • 04 93 61 20 37 • DA • €€€€*

7 La Coupole, Hôtel Mirabeau, Monaco
Elegant restaurant with a new interpretation of local dishes such as *socca (see p51)*. 🛇 *1 ave Princesse Grace • Map H4 • 03 77 92 16 65 • DA • €€€€*

8 Le Cagnard, Cagnes-sur-Mer
The restaurant of this hideaway hotel is highly regarded for dishes such as black truffle lasagne. 🛇 *Rue Sous-Barri • Map G4 • 04 93 20 73 21 • DA • €€€*

9 Le Vistamar, Monaco
Mediterranean decor and a fine menu, dominated by superb seafood. 🛇 *Hôtel l'Hermitage, sq Beaumarchais • Map H4 • 03 77 92 16 40 00 • No vegetarian options • DA • €€€€*

10 Josy Jo, Haute-de-Cagnes
Ivy-covered restaurant in a pretty village, serving grilled meat Provençale style. 🛇 *2 rue du Planastel • Map G4 • 04 93 20 68 76 • Closed Sat L, Sun • No vegetarian options • €€*

Josy Jo, Haute-de-Cagnes

Note: *Unless otherwise stated, all restaurants accept credit cards and serve vegetarian meals*

103

Left **Mosaic, Musée Fernand Léger, Biot** Right **Grasse**

Alpes-Maritimes

TECHNICALLY, THE RIVIERA IS PART OF *the Alpes-Maritimes département,
but inland from the coastal highway the landscape changes dramatically
and the region's forested mountains, deep river gorges and medieval hilltop
villages seem a million miles from the busy seaside resorts. High in the
mountains is the Parc National du Mercantour, a region of rocky summits
and glaciers which shelters chamois, ibex and rare lammergeier vultures. In
winter heavy snowfall makes this one of France's favourite ski areas.*

🔟 Sights

1. Vence
2. Vallée des Merveilles & Musée des Merveilles
3. Fondation Maeght, St-Paul-de-Vence
4. Biot
5. Gorges du Cians
6. Forêt de Turini
7. Gorges du Loup
8. Grasse
9. Vallée de la Vesubie
10. La Trophée des Alpes

Alpes-Maritimes landscape

1 Vence

A gem of the region, with an unbeatable location on a high crag and sweeping views. The old medieval centre is ringed by formidable battlement walls and is entered through a massive stone gateway, to a labyrinth of cobbled streets and tall stone houses. A small cathedral, dating from the 11th century, stands on place Clemenceau. ◈ Map G4

Chagall painting, Fondation Maeght

2 Vallée des Merveilles and Musée des Merveilles

High in the Parc National de Mercantour (see p40), this valley shelters a treasury of Bronze Age art (see p60). Rock carvings are scattered over the barren slopes of the 2,870-m (9,400-ft) Mont Bégo, and date from 1800–1500 BC. They are almost impossible to find without a guide, but the less energetic can see fascinating examples in the excellent Musée des Merveilles at Tende. ◈ Map H2 • Musée des Merveilles: ave du 16 Septembre 1947, Tende, Open May–15 Oct: 10am-6:30pm Wed–Mon, 16 Oct–Apr: 10am–5pm, Adm

3 Fondation Maeght, St-Paul-de-Vence

One of the finest small modern art museums in the world, the Maeght Foundation includes work by Marc Chagall, Joan Miró, Fernand Léger, Alberto Giacometti and many more 20th-century artists. The collection is exhibited in rotation, and the only works on permanent display are the large sculptures which surround the museum (see p34). ◈ Route de Pass-Prest • Map G4 • Open Jul–Sep: 10am–7pm; Oct–Jun: 10am–12:30pm, 2:30–6pm daily • Adm

4 Biot

Only minutes from the crowded beaches of Antibes and Juan-les-Pins and the busy coastal highway, Biot sits serenely on a hilltop among pinewoods. This pretty little town was once known for its pottery and is now renowned for its high-quality decorative glassware, which you can watch being blown at La Verrerie de Biot, just outside the village. The modern Musée Fernand Léger contains more than 400 drawings and paintings by the artist (see p34). ◈ Map G4 • Musée Fernand Leger: chemin du Val-de-Pome, Open 10am–12:30pm, 2–5:30pm Wed–Mon, Adm • La Verrerie de Biot: chemin des Combes, Open 9am–noon, 2–5pm Mon–Sat, Adm

Fondation Maeght

Vallée de la Vesubie

slopes in semi-tropical luxuriance and huge pines rise on the higher mountainsides. From Pointe des Trois Communes, on the fringe of the forest at an altitude of 2,082 m (6,830 ft), there is a quite breathtaking panorama of the Alpine foothills and the Parc National de Mercantour *(see p40)*. Ⓢ *Map H3*

5 Gorges du Cians
The deep gorge carved through the mountains by the River Cians is made all the more spectacular by the deep red of the exposed rock. The river descends 1,600 m (5,250 ft) in just 25 km (15 miles) between the eyrie village of Beuil and Touet-sur-Var, where the Cians meets the larger river Var. The canyon is at its narrowest and most spectacular at Pra d'Astier, around midway between the two villages *(see p41)*. Ⓢ *Map G3*

6 Forêt de Turini
A moist micro-climate, created by warm sea air rising over the cooler mountains, waters this mountain forest, where thick beech, maple and chestnut woods cloak the lower

Skiing in the Alpes d'Azur

High above the balmy coast, the summits and slopes of the Alpes d'Azur are deeply covered in snow in winter, with excellent skiing conditions, and there are more than 250 pistes, ranging from black to green runs, in well-equipped resorts. The best known is Isola 2000, with 5 black runs, 14 red, 13 blue and 4 green, suitable for skiers of all levels.

7 Gorges du Loup
The most spectacular of the region's river canyons. Here the River Loup has sliced its way deep into the limestone rock to create a series of waterfalls including the 40-m (130-ft) Cascade de Courmes, churning rapids and deep potholes such as the Saut du Loup *(see p41)*. Ⓢ *Map G3*

8 Grasse
Grasse is a rather unpre-possessing town at first sight, but its air is scented by the perfume factories for which it has been famous for more than four centuries. Vast quantities of blossoms are processed here for their essential oils, and a jasmine festival is held each year in August. You can find out how perfume is made at the Musée Internationale de la Parfumerie *(see p54)*. Ⓢ *Map G4 • Musée Internationale de la Parfumerie: 8 place du Cours, Open 9am–noon, 2–5:30pm daily (Closed Tue Oct–May), Adm*

9 Vallée de la Vésubie
Two streams merge at St-Martin-Vésubie to form the River Vesubie, which flows through landscapes of pinewoods, flower meadows, forested peaks and narrow canyons to join the Var

Grasse

24 km (15 miles) north of Nice. The valley is dotted with attractive villages, and the river is at its most scenic where it passes through the Gorges de la Vesubie, a canyon of coloured rock walls. ◉ *Map H3*

10 La Trophée des Alpes

Also known as the Trophée d'Auguste, this remarkable Roman monument is the only building of its kind still in existence. Its towering columns can be seen from afar and there are views along the Riviera. A museum shows a video about the monument's history *(see p30)*. ◉ *Ave Albert 1er, La Turbie • Open Apr–20 Jun 9:30am–6pm daily, 21 Jun–20 Sep: 9:30am–7pm daily, 21 Sep–Mar: 10am–5:30pm Tue–Sun • Adm*

La Trophée des Alpes

A Walk through Medieval Vence

A giant ash tree, Le Frêne (The Ash) is your landmark for the beginning of this two-hour stroll through the old quarter of **Vence** *(see p105)*, with its stone-paved streets and medieval houses huddling inside a ring of 13th-century battlements. Before entering the walls through the 16th-century Porte de Peyra, visit the Château de Villeneuve, which hosts a changing programme of contemporary art and design exhibitions.

After walking through the gateway, turn right, and allow half an hour to walk along the rue du Marché, where the rows of shops selling herbs, fruit, fresh pasta and fish will make your mouth water. At the end of the rue du Marché, turn left and walk across place Surian and place Clemenceau to the cathedral – look out for Roman inscriptions dating back almost 2,000 years on the masonry of the buildings either side of it, carved when Vence was the Roman settlement of Vintium. Also look for the oak choir stalls carved with little satirical figures, commissioned by a witty 17th-century bishop.

Leave the square by its north side, through the arched Passage Cahors, then walk up rue du Seminaire and turn left to follow the old walls along rue de la Coste. Leave the old quarter by the Portail Levis, which takes you back on to place du Frêne. There are several cafés and restaurants here, such as **Auberge des Seigneurs** *(see p109)* where you can enjoy a drink and snack.

Left **Gourdon** Right **Peillon**

🔟 Mountain Villages

1 St-Paul-de-Vence
The prettiest and best known of the region's *villages perchés* (see p78), St-Paul was first built as a refuge from Saracen raiders. From its ramparts there are terrific views down to the sea (see p38). ◈ Map G4

2 Puget-Théniers
Puget-Théniers stands where the Roudoule river meets the Var, overlooked by the ruins of the Château des Grimaldi (see p93). The Romanesque church has a beautiful 16th-century altarpiece (see p33). ◈ Map G3

3 St-Cézaire
This hill village has been settled since the Roman era and has medieval walls and watch towers. Nearby are the grottoes of St-Cézaire, an underground wonderland. ◈ Map G3 • Grottes de St-Cézaire-sur-Siagne: rte de Grasse, Open Jun & Sep: 10:30am–noon, 2–6pm, Jul–Aug: 10:30am–6.30pm, Oct–Nov: 2:30–5pm daily, Adm

4 Gourdon
From the village square, where the hillside drops into a limestone gorge, you can see all the way down the Loup valley to the coast. ◈ Map G3

5 Peillon
Peillon's red-tiled houses seem to grow out of the hilltop itself,

rising in tiers to a cobbled square with great views of the forested valley. It seems barely changed since the Middle Ages. ◈ Map H3

6 Sospel
Colourful arcaded houses and a Baroque church are features of this pretty mountain village near the Italian border. Badly damaged in World War II, it has been lovingly restored. ◈ Map H3

7 Luceram
Here, tall old houses are set around a 17th-century rococo church and an onion-domed clock tower. ◈ Map H3

8 Saorge
The clifftop location rivals Gourdon's for dizzying effect, and the village is a little changed crescent of 15th–17th-century pastel houses. It has two pretty churches, and magnificent views. ◈ Map H3

9 La Brigue
Unspoilt La Brigue has cobbled streets, arcaded buildings and the Notre-Dame-des-Fontaines with its superb medieval frescoes. ◈ Map G2

10 St-Agnès
At 671 m (2,200 ft) St-Agnès is the highest of the coastal *villages perchés*. There is fine walking nearby, in the Gorbio valley. ◈ Map H3

Statue, Puget-Théniers

Price Categories

For a three-course
meal for one with half
a bottle of wine (or
equivalent meal), taxes
and extra charges.

€ under €30
€€ €30–40
€€€ €40–50
€€€€ €50–60
€€€€€ over €60

Left **Auberge de la Madone, Peillon**

10 Places to Eat

1 Auberge de la Madone, Peillon

Delightfully located just outside the village, with immaculate white linen under shading vines on the terrace, this *auberge* specializes in local dishes. ⊗ *Map H3 • 04 93 79 91 17 • Closed Wed • €€€*

2 Bastide St-Antoine, Grasse

For once, a restaurant with real vegetarian options, such as asparagus in anise and olive oil or melon with tomatoes. Great for carnivores too. ⊗ *48 ave Henri Dunant • Map G4 • 04 93 09 16 48 • DA • €€€€*

3 Le St-Paul, St-Paul-de-Vence

Attached to a gorgeous hideaway hotel, Le St-Paul serves fine seafood and other dishes on a terrace with views from the village battlements, or in a gracious dining room. ⊗ *86 rue Grande • Map G4 • 04 93 32 65 25 • €€€€*

4 Auberge du Jarrier, Biot

Hidden away in a side street, this restaurant offers value for money and has a pretty terrace. ⊗ *30 passage de la Bourgade • Map G4 • 04 93 65 11 68 • Closed Mon, Mar • No vegetarian options • €€€*

5 Auberge des Seigneurs, Vence

Freshly caught trout and spit-roasted local lamb are among the choices at this friendly medieval inn on the edge of the old quarter, complete with open fire. ⊗ *Pl du Frêne • Map G4 • 04 93 58 04 24 • Closed Mon, Tue–Wed L, Nov–Feb • No vegetarian options • DA • €*

6 Le Nid d'Aigle, Gourdon

Lots of different rooms and a terrace, all with views that justify the name "Eagle's Nest". ⊗ *Pl Victoria • Map G3 • 04 93 77 52 02 • Closed D Jan–mid-Feb • No vegetarian options • DA • €*

7 Maximin, Vence

Elegant restaurant with a menu prepared by masterchef Jacques Maximin – simple ingredients but sophisticated recipes. ⊗ *689 chemin de la Gaude • Map G4 • 04 93 58 90 75 • Closed Mon–Tue • No vegetarian options • DA • €€€€€*

8 Les Templiers, Vence

Another gourmet choice, with dishes such as tagliatelle with cepes and truffles. Dinner only. ⊗ *39 ave Joffre • Map G4 • 04 93 58 06 05 • €€*

9 La Farigoule, Vence

Unpretentious restaurant with an array of seafood, meat and vegetarian dishes. ⊗ *15 ave Henri-Isnard • Map G4 • 04 93 58 01 27 • Closed Tue–Wed • €€*

10 Hostellerie Jerome, La Turbie

Inventive dishes such as pigeon with olives and cepes. Dinner only. ⊗ *20 rue Comte de Cessole • Map H3 • 04 92 41 51 51 • Closed Mon–Tue • €€*

Note: *Unless otherwise stated, all restaurants accept credit cards and serve vegetarian meals*

Left **Rocky landscape outside Sisteron** Right **Lavender fields, Valensole**

Alpes-de-Haute-Provence

ONE OF THE HIGHEST AND WILDEST PARTS OF FRANCE, *and indeed Europe, Alpes-de-Haute-Provence presents a sharp contrast to the foothills and valleys of the Var to the south and the rolling Vaucluse to the west. Summers are hot, winters are bitterly cold and life in these harsh mountains is hard – which is why so much of Haute-Provence is sparsely inhabited. The Durance river flows through the region to meet the Rhône north of Aix, and tributaries such as the Verdon cut spectacular gorges through the limestone rock of the mountains, adding to the breathtaking views, cool clear air and pocket wildernesses of this beautiful region. The area also offers a range of sports from white-water canoeing, to hang-gliding, to high-country walking.*

Sights

1. Parc Naturel Régional du Verdon
2. Citadelle de Sisteron
3. Mont Pelat
4. Fort de Savoie, Colmars
5. Lurs
6. Ville Forte, Entrevaux
7. Moustiers-Sainte-Marie
8. Musée de la Préhistoire des Gorges du Verdon
9. Montagne de Lure
10. Forcalquier

Moustiers-Sainte-Marie

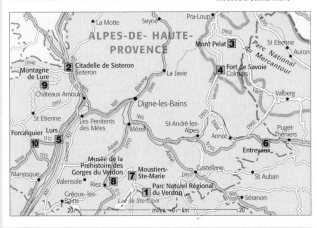

1 Parc Naturel Régional du Verdon

Along the river Verdon, this national park is a huge patchwork of landscapes from the neatly cultivated lavender fields of the sunlit Valensole plateau *(see p55)* to the forested hills and pastures of the Artuby, the awesome chasms of the Grand Canyon du Verdon *(see pp10–11)* and the beginnings of the Alps. There are brilliant blue lakes created where the Verdon has been dammed. This is a paradise for hikers, with a network of 700 km (450 miles) of paths, bridleways and ancient mule highways. ◈ *Map E3*

2 Citadelle de Sisteron

Squatting on a steep-sided crag, high above the narrow valley of the River Durance, the formidable defences of the Citadelle guard one of the strategic gateways to Provence *(see p39)*. Built in the 13th century, the bastions and ramparts, crowned by towers and a graceful chapel, are an awesome piece of military engineering. In summer, they become the venue for the Nuits de la Citadelle, an enchanting festival of music, theatre and dance. ◈ *Pl de la Citadelle • Map E2 • Open mid-Mar–mid-Nov: 9am–sunset daily • Adm*

Citadelle de Sisteron

3 Mont Pelat

The highest peak in the Provençal Alps rises to a height of 3,050 m (10,020 ft) and dominates a lofty landscape of bare rocky summits, streaked by snow until early summer, pine forests and alpine meadows. The massif is crossed by breathtaking passes, including the Cime de la Bonette, by which the D64 road traverses the shoulder of Mont Pelat at a height of 2,860 m (9,400 ft), making it the highest pass in Europe. ◈ *Map F2*

4 Fort de Savoie, Colmars

This 17th-century fortress has a grim, businesslike look when compared with the fairytale medieval castles found elsewhere in Provence. It was built to withstand cannon fire, not just arrows and siege towers. The work of the master military

Fort de Savoie, Colmars

engineer Vauban, it is a remarkable testimony to his skill. The Fort de France, the second of this former frontier garrison's strongholds, has fared less well and lies in ruins. ◈ *Map F2 • Open Jul–Aug: 9am–noon daily for guided tours; Sep–Jun: by appt • Adm*

5 Lurs

Founded before the reign of Charlemagne, during the Dark Ages, the town of Lurs was fortified as early as the 9th century AD, when it was ruled by the bishops of Sisteron and the princes of Lurs. Deserted in the 19th century, it has now become an artists' colony known for prints and graphic arts. There are stupendous views from the Promenade des Evêques (Bishops' Walk) leading to the chapel of Notre-Dame-de-Vie, especially colourful in spring when the wildflowers bloom. ◈ *Map D2*

6 Ville Forte, Entrevaux

Only a brave or foolhardy enemy would have attempted to assail the citadel of Entrevaux, one of the most dramatic of all the region's many fortresses. Perched on a pinnacle above the fairytale town, it can be reached only by a zig-zag path which passes through more than a dozen arched gateways. Lying beneath it, the impregnable Ville

Napoleon at Sisteron

On 1 March 1815 Napoleon Bonaparte escaped from exile on Elba and landed at Golfe Juan. Had the citadel at Sisteron been garrisoned by Royalist troops, his attempt to regain his Imperial throne might have been foiled, but he entered the town unopposed on 5 March to begin a triumphal progress to Paris, only to meet final defeat at Waterloo.

Entrevaux citadel

Forte is ringed by towers and ramparts and reached by a drawbridge. ◈ *Map F3*

7 Moustiers-Sainte-Marie

Moustiers, loud with the sound of a swift-running stream which flows through the middle of the village, is simply delightful, with its tall old houses, shady plane trees and flower baskets and, for those who can face the climb, a superb view of the Gorges du Verdon from the clifftop church of Notre-Dame-de-Beauvoir *(see p32)*. The village was and is famed for its faïence ware, and you can see wonderful examples in the Musée de la Faïence *(see p38)*. ◈ *Map E3 • Musée de la Faïence: rue Bourgade, Open Dec–Oct: 9am–noon, 2–6pm Wed–Mon, Nov: 2–5pm Sat–Sun, Adm*

8 Musée de la Préhistoire des Gorges du Verdon

This new museum, in a building designed by British architect Norman Foster, retraces the geological, cultural and environmental evolution of human life in the Verdon and throughout Europe, with an imaginative and fascinating series of displays and interactive exhibits. Guided visits to the caves, where relics of early humans have been discovered, are also offered. ◈ *Le Village 04500 Quinson • Map E3 • Open Feb–mid-Dec: 10am–6pm Wed–Mon • Adm*

9 Montagne de Lure
Deep in the heart of the Luberon, the Lure mountain – an extension of the savage massif of Mont Ventoux in neighbouring Vaucluse *(see p117)* – is Provence at its wildest, least hospitable and, some would say, its loveliest. Abandoned hamlets are reminders of Provence in the first half of the 20th century, when many rural people gave up trying to scrape a living from this harsh countryside. ◈ *Map D2*

10 Forcalquier
Forcalquier is a beguiling old town, evocative of past glories, when it was the seat of powerful local lords and capital of the region. One gate of the old walled

Scriptorium, Couvent des Cordeliers

town, the Porte des Cordeliers, still survives, along with the restored cloisters and stark library of the 13th-century Couvent des Cordeliers, with its tombs of the town's medieval *seigneurs*. ◈ *Map D3 • Couvent des Cordeliers: blvd des Martyrs, Open May–Jun, mid-Sep–Oct: 2–5pm; Jul–mid-Sep: 9am–noon, 2–5pm Sun for guided tours, Adm*

A Morning Drive through the Canyon

🕐 Start after breakfast from the unassuming town of **Castellane** *(see p114)*, gateway to the canyons, and drive west on D952. The landscape becomes progressively more awe-inspiring as you enter the gorges and wind your way through towering walls of rock to **Point Sublime** *(see p10)*. This is one of the most impressive viewpoints; savour it while enjoying a coffee or a cold drink at the pleasant **Auberge du Point Sublime** *(see p115)*.

From here, drive for about 15 minutes and turn left on to the vertiginous Route des Crêtes, which winds past a series of ever higher viewpoints. Don't rush this part of the drive, but stop at each for five or ten minutes, as the views vary all the time. Finally, the road swings around the shoulder of the massif, and far below you is the Verdon and the plateau country around the little village of **La-Palud-sur-Verdon** *(see p114)*. It will take you another 30 minutes to get there, so relax when you do with another coffee at one of the village restaurants.

From Le-Palud it's a less daunting drive until the gorgeous turquoise waters of the **Lac de Ste-Croix** *(see p10)* come into sight. The road runs high above the lake, bringing you to the delightfully pretty village of **Moustiers-Ste-Marie**. Reward yourself with lunch here: the village has two of the region's best restaurants, **La Treille Muscat** and **Les Santons** *(see p115)*.

Left **Seyne-les-Alpes countryside** Right **Bar, Castellane**

Towns and Villages

1 Les Mées
Tucked away in the hills, the little village of Les Mées is best known for the strange rock formations known as the Pénitents des Mées. Legend says these pinnacles were once monks who broke their vows of chastity and were turned to stone by St Donat *(see p60)*. ✎ *Map E3*

2 Simiane-la-Rotonde
The enigmatic Rotonde, a Roman relic whose purpose is still a puzzle, crowns the village to which it lends its name, a picturesque cluster of old houses and churches protected by a ramshackle medieval fort. ✎ *Map E3*

3 Seyne-les-Alpes
Military and religious architecture are scattered throughout this quiet mountain town: a 15th-century gate, a medieval church and a ruined citadel are the main points of interest. ✎ *Map E2*

4 Annot
Annot stands in unspoilt countryside in the Vaire valley. Many houses are built into the giant sandstone glacial boulders, known as the *grès d'Annot* – some have 17th- and 18th-century carved façades. ✎ *Map F3*

5 La-Palud-sur-Verdon
La-Palud stands on the north side of the Grand Canyon du Verdon, making it a popular base for exploring the region *(see pp10–11)*. ✎ *Map E3*

6 Castellane
Castellane is a lively market town surrounded by steep mountains. The Verdon flows through it on its way to the Grand Canyon. It is also a centre for adventure sports *(see p11)*. ✎ *Map E3*

7 Allemagne en Provence
Allemagne en Provence stands between the rugged canyon country of the Verdon and the lavender fields of the Valensole plateau. It is dominated by the palatial Château d'Allemagne, founded in the 12th century, which is now a luxury guesthouse *(see p143)*. ✎ *Map E3*

8 St-André-les-Alpes
This little village bustles in summer. Built where the Verdon and Isolde rivers flow into the manmade Lac de Castillon, it is a popular watersports centre, with dinghies, windsurfers and canoes for hire. ✎ *Map F3*

9 Beauvezer
Beauvezer, in the dramatic Vallée du Haut Verdon, stands 1,179 m (3,600 ft) above sea level. Once a frontier fortress, it still has its formidable battlements. ✎ *Map E3*

10 Barcelonnette
Provence's northernmost town stands in the rugged Ubaye valley. High in the Alps, its cobbled streets are ringed by peaks that have a scattering of snow until June. ✎ *Map F1*

Above **La Treille Muscat, Moustiers-Ste-Marie**

🔟 Places to Eat

1 Le Grand Paris, Digne

The restaurant of Digne's best hotel, a renovated convent, serves solid regional cooking such as terrine of lentils with pâté de foie gras. ✎ *Hôtel du Grand Paris, 19 blvd Thiers • Map E2 • 04 92 31 11 15 • No vegetarian options • DA • €€*

2 La Bonne Etape, Château-Amoux

In this otherwise dull town, La Bonne Etape features Provençale cuisine at its best with dishes such as stuffed courgette (zucchini) flowers and local lamb. ✎ *Chemin du Lac • Map E3 • 04 92 64 00 09 • No vegetarian options • €€€€*

3 La Treille Muscat, Moustiers-Ste-Marie

Excellent food such as pistou of summer vegetables in this lovely hotel, with a terrace overlooking the stream. ✎ *Pl de l'Eglise • Map E3 • 04 92 74 64 31 • DA • €€*

4 Les Santons, Moustiers-Ste-Marie

Next door to La Treille Muscat is this pretty restaurant with a leafy terrace, serving gastronomic dishes. ✎ *Pl de l'Eglise • Map E3 • 04 92 74 66 48 • No vegetarian options • €€*

5 Hostellerie de la Fuste, Valensole

Award-winning meals prepared from home-grown produce, fresh fish and local lamb, in the heart of the lavender fields. ✎ *La Fuste • Map E3 • 04 92 72 05 95 • No vegetarian options • DA • €€*

6 Ferme-Auberge Le Bas Chalus, Forcalquier

A wonderful, simple inn serving typical dishes of the region, simply prepared. ✎ *Rte de Niozelles • Map D3 • 04 92 75 05 67 • No vegetarian options • €*

7 Le Verdon, Gréoux-les-Bains

Very good value for money, with dishes such as Alpine lamb with Valensole honey or baked ham with foie gras. There's also a pleasant terrace. ✎ *Quartier des Hautes Plaines • Map E3 • 02 43 71 36 18 • No vegetarian options • €*

8 Auberge du Point Sublime, Rougon

The location makes this inn special, with a terrace gazing out at the peaks of the Canyon du Verdon. The food is reasonable. ✎ *Point Sublime • Map E3 • 04 92 83 60 35 • Closed mid-Oct–Mar • €*

9 Bello Visto, Lurs

This restaurant specializes in unusual combinations of meat and fruits with dishes such as pork in figs. ✎ *Le Village • Map D3 • 04 92 79 95 09 • No vegetarian options • €*

10 Le Vieux Colombier, Dabisse les Mées

Close to the rock formations of Les Mées, the terrace of this charming inn, in a converted dovecote, is a lovely place to sample dishes such as pigeon in truffle sauce. ✎ *RD 4 • Map E3 • 04 92 34 32 32 • DA • €€*

Note: Unless otherwise stated, all restaurants accept credit cards and serve vegetarian meals

115

Left **Pont St-Bénézet, Avignon** Right **Roman theatre, Orange**

Vaucluse

AT THE NORTHERN GATES OF PROVENCE, *the Vaucluse exudes a cultured air. Its rich past – Roman inheritance in Orange, papal legacy in Avignon – is amplified by summer festivals in both towns, while the perched villages of the Luberon seem purpose-built for holiday homes. But the villages are not perched by accident and Avignon's ramparts were not for show – defence was the motive for both. On Mont Ventoux, the Monts de Vaucluse or remote parts of the Luberon, you're in Provence at its most elemental.*

Sights

Avignon

1 Vaison-la-Romaine

One of the best preserved Roman towns in Provence *(see pp22–3)*.

2 Abbaye de Sénanque

When the summer lavender flowers, this medieval abbey surrounded by purple fields is a spectacular sight *(see pp24–5)*.

3 Mont Ventoux

The bald-headed "Giant of Provence" is the Vaucluse's greatest landmark, a vast pyramid of rock which has inspired poets, mystics and botanists for centuries. Rising 1,900 m (6,300 ft), it commands the surrounding landscape, affording astonishing views to the sea, the Alps and the Rhône. Snow-capped in winter, the summit is revealed as arid chalk in summer and buffeted by strong winds all year round. The lower slopes are dense with trees, 1,000 plant varieties and wildlife. ◎ *Map C2*

4 Roman Theatre, Orange

The finest Roman theatre in Europe still has its original stage wall, 106 m (350 ft) long, 36 m (120 ft) high and guaranteeing perfect acoustics *(see p30)*. ◎ *Pl des Frères-Mounet • Map B2 • Open 9am–6:30pm daily • Adm*

5 Parc Naturel Régional du Luberon

The Luberon has a wild, mountain beauty and it is the park's job to maintain the balance between tourists and the environment. Covering 150,000 ha (375,000 acres), it takes in the

Vaison-la-Romaine

Augustus statue, Orange

rugged Petit Luberon of crags, gorges and perched villages to the west and the more rounded Grand Luberon to the east. It also stretches north to the Monts de Vaucluse. The park's headquarters in Apt have information on walks, the ecology and the area's traditions. Sheep grazing is, for instance, vital to maintaining heathlands *(see p40)*. ◎ *Maison du Parc, 60 pl Jean-Jaurès • Map C3 • Open 8:30am–npon, 1:30–6pm Mon–Fri, 8:30am–noon Sat • Free*

6 Gorges de la Nesque

Second only to the Verdon gorges *(see pp10–11)* in dramatic potential, the Nesque gorges run for 20 km (12 miles) between the villages of Villes-sur-Auzon and Monieux. The rocky drop descends more than 300 m (1,000 ft), its sides alternately bare or covered in scrub vegetation. Cut into the cliff, the winding road is not for vertigo sufferers. The Castelleras viewpoint looks onto the 850-m (2,800-ft) Rocher de Cire (Wax Rock – so-called because it is home to millions of bees). This is also the start of a

Fontaine-de-Vaucluse

World War II and another equally good one devoted to speleology (caves and caving). ◈ *Map C3*
• *Petrarch Museum: Rive gauche de la Sorgue, Open Wed–Mon, Adm • Museum d'Histoire: Chemin du Gouffre, Open Wed–Mon DA, Adm • Speleology Museum: Chemin du Gouffre, Open daily, DA, Adm*

testing walk to the bottom of the gorges, where Chapel St-Michel is dug into the rock. ◈ *Map C3*

7 Fontaine-de-Vaucluse

From the base of grandiose, 230-m (750-ft) high cliffs, Europe's most powerful spring pumps out the water which creates the River Sorgue. The romance and mystery of the setting (no one has yet found the exact source of the water) attracts millions of visitors every year, as it once attracted 14th-century Italian poet Petrarch *(see p38)*. Downstream of the source, the charming little village celebrates its most famous inhabitant with a museum in one of the houses claimed to have been his. It also boasts an excellent museum dedicated to the history, art and literature of

---

The Vaudois Massacre

The bloodiest tale in Provençal history took place in Vaucluse in 1545, when Catholic Royal authorities determined to exterminate early Protestant settlers, the Vaudois. Within weeks as many as 3,000 were dead: women and children were burned alive and villages were destroyed. The memories, and ruins, still haunt the remoter mountainsides.

---

8 Les Dentelles de Montmirail

Probably the prettiest mountain range in Provence, the Dentelles are formed by three ridges of chalk topped by ragged crests. The French think of these as lacework *(dentelles)*, but they can look more like fangs in rough weather. Within the range, tiny villages (Suzette, La Roque Alric) cling to the crags as if by magic and climbers are attracted to the sheer rock-faces. The walking, too, is spectacularly good, notably up to St Amand, at 730 m (2,400 ft), the highest point. Round the western edge cluster the picturesque wine villages of Beaumes-de-Venise, Gigondas, Vacqueyras and Séguret. It's advisable to stop here after, rather than before, a ramble *(see pp52–3)*. ◈ *Map C2*

9 Synagogue, Carpentras

Expelled from France in the 14th century, the Jews sought refuge in those parts of Provence then belonging to the pope. This included Carpentras, whose synagogue, founded in 1367, is the oldest still functioning on French soil. Rebuilt in the 18th century, the synagogue looks like neighbouring buildings from the outside: laws forbade decoration.

Within, the ground floor and cellar boasts the old bakery (for unleavened bread) and pools essential for Jewish rituals. These are presently being restored. A monumental staircase leads to the sumptuous two-storey area of worship (men upstairs, women below), setting for the tabernacle, teba, candelabra and magnificent chandeliers. ✆ *Pl de la Mairie • Map C3 • Open 10am–noon, 3–5pm Mon–Fri (until 4pm Fri) • Donation*

10 **Cathédrale St-Anne, Apt**
The relics of St Anne (mother of the Virgin) were apparently discovered on this site in 776. They're still here, having survived the destruction of the church and its rebuilding from the 11th century on. The two crypts have also survived, containing sarcophagi from earliest Christian times. The cathedral is rich in 18th-century paintings and a splendid 15th-century stained-glass window of the Tree of Jesse. The 17th-century St Anne Chapel contains what is said to be the saint's veil, although it's probably of 9th-century Egyptian origin. ✆ *Rue St-Anne • Map C3 • Open 10am–noon, 3–6pm Tue–Sat • Free*

Vaucluse vineyards

A Day's Drive in the Vaucluse Mountains

Morning

🕐 Start in Carpentras by visiting the **synagogue**. Take the D942 to Mazan and on, through woodland, to Villes-sur-Auzon, a charming Provençal village. Continue on the D942 to the **Gorges de la Nesque** *(see p117)* to experience 20 km (12 miles) of awe-inspiring scenery, with sheer drops of 300 m (1,000 ft). Pause at the Belvédère de Castelleras for heart-stopping views.

🍴 Continue to Monieux, stopping at Les Lavandes restaurant in the village centre *(04 90 64 05 08 • €)* if it is time for lunch and you fancy savoury, rustic cooking. Continue to **Sault** *(see p54)* where, in July and August, the valley is a riot of purple lavender, yellow broom and the white of the rocks – an unmissable sight.

Afternoon

Take the D164 towards **Mont Ventoux** *(see p117)*, another challenging drive, and stop for breaks at Col des Tempêtes for the views across Toulourenc Valley, then the summit for the most stunning panorama in Provence.

🍷 Descend the mountain to Malaucène, taking the tiny D90 into the **Dentelles de Montmirail**. Pause in any of the cafés in Beaumes-de-Venise for a glass of the local sweet white wine. Continue to delightful **Séguret** *(see p39)*, then return by the D7 to Carpentras, rewarding yourself 🍴 with dinner at Le Vert Galant *(12 rue de Clapies, 04 90 67 15 50 • €€)*, the best restaurant in town.

Following pages **St-Paul-de-Vence**

119

Around Provence – Vaucluse

Left **Place de l'Horloge** Right **Vièrge de Pitié, Musée du Petit Palais**

Avignon Sights

1 Palais des Papes
The medieval papal palace dominates the town *(see pp8–9)*.

2 Cathédrale Notre-Dame-des-Doms
The medieval popes' cathedral. The building underwent alteration in the 17th century, but retains a 13th-century altar. ⚲ *Pl du Palais • Map B3 • Open 7am–7pm daily • Free*

3 Pont St-Bénézet
The 13th-century bridge once had 22 arches across the Rhône. Flood damage has reduced it to just four arches which stop mid-stream *(see p60)*. ⚲ *Rue Ferruce • Map B3 • Open 9am–6pm daily • Adm*

4 Musée Calvet
One of provincial France's finest museums, with collections from ancient Greece to the 20th century. ⚲ *65 rue Joseph Vernet • Map B3 • Open 10am–1pm, 2–6pm Wed–Mon • Adm*

Gardens, Cathédrale Notre-Dame-des-Doms

5 Rue des Teinturiers
The tiny street used to be home to dye-workers (hence the waterwheels). It now buzzes with arty cafés. ⚲ *Map B3*

6 Place de l'Horloge
Built on the old forum, the city's nerve centre is fringed with restaurants, bars and the 19th-century town hall. ⚲ *Map B3*

7 Musée Angladon-Dubrujeaud
This private collection includes works by Cézanne, Manet, Picasso, and the only Van Gogh painting permanently exhibited in Provence. ⚲ *5 rue Labourer • Map B3 • Open 1–6pm Wed– Sun • Adm*

8 Musée du Petit Palais
One of Europe's finest museums of medieval and Renaissance art, with exceptional early works by Botticelli. ⚲ *Pl du Palais • Map B3 • Open Jun–Sep: 10am–1pm, 2–6pm; Oct–May: 9:30am–1pm, 2–5:30pm Wed–Mon • Adm*

9 Chartreuse du Val-de-Bénédiction
Elegant gardens and a splendid chapel make this one of the most impressive monasteries in France. ⚲ *Rue de la République • Map B3 • Open 9:30am–5:30pm daily • Adm*

10 Collection Lambert
Avignon's premier showcase for contemporary art. ⚲ *Hôtel de Caumont, 5 rue Violette • Map B3 • Open 11am–7pm Tue–Sun • Adm*

Around Provence – Vaucluse

Left **Gordes** Right **Château d'Ansouis, Ansouis**

TOP10 Vaucluse Villages

1 Roussillon
Ochre mining and erosion have fashioned the multicoloured earth into cliffs and fantastic shapes, creating a bewitching setting for a romantic perched village *(see p39)*. ◈ *Map C3*

2 Séguret
This remarkable medieval settlement hugs its hillside like a tight belt *(see p39)*. ◈ *Map C3*

3 Gordes
Fashionable folk flock here, and no wonder. The village is perched above the Coulon Valley, and its little houses appear piled on top of one another. In the centre, the chateau oversees the whole with Renaissance dignity. ◈ *Map C3*

4 Oppède-le-Vieux
Flourishing in Renaissance times, Oppède was deserted by 1900 – no one wanted to live on a barely accessible rock. Now some of the houses are being restored but the spot remains profoundly atmospheric, with medieval castle ruins. ◈ *Map C3*

5 Brantes
Overhanging the gorges 550 m (1,800 ft) below, Brantes stares across the Toulourenc Valley to Mont Ventoux. Its tiny paved streets and vaulted passages boast a chapel but no shops. It is particularly impressive in March, when the almond trees are in bloom. ◈ *Map C2*

6 Ansouis
This village, with its wandering little streets, is made truly remarkable by its chateau, built in the 12th century and still lived in by descendants of the same family. The vaulted rooms, armoury, salons and, especially, the kitchens are extraordinary. ◈ *Map C3 • Chateau: rue Coquette, Open 2.30–6pm daily, Adm*

7 Ménerbes
Ménerbes was superbly sited for defence. As a Protestant stronghold, it held out for five years during the 16th-century Wars of Religion. The position remains dramatic, but peace now reigns around the citadel and townhouses. The views are terrific. ◈ *Map C3*

8 Malaucène
This was where Pope Clement V had his summer residence, and it remains a graceful spot of 17th- and 18th-century houses, fountains and avenues shaded by plane trees. ◈ *Map C3*

9 Vacqueyras
One of Provence's most prestigious wine villages. Note the 11th-century church with its elegant belltower, then go to taste the wine. ◈ *Map C3*

10 Le Barroux
An eagle's nest of a village, its narrow streets lead steeply up to the splendid chateau at the top. ◈ *Map C3*

For Provence's Top 10 villages **See pp38–9**

Left **L'Isle-sur-la-Sorgue** Right **Printed fabrics, Les Olivades**

TOP10 Shops in Vaucluse

1 L'Isle-sur-la-Sorgue
Not one shop but more than 200 make this little town France's most important antiques and second-hand centre after Paris. Grouped into seven centres, most are open Saturday to Monday, with a market on Sunday mornings. Antiques fairs at Easter and around 15 August. ◎ *Map C3*

2 Peasant Market, Velleron
Provence isn't short of food markets, but this one is special. It's held in the evening and stall-holders must sell homegrown or raised produce only. Monday to Saturday from 6pm, April to September and Tuesday, Wednesday, Friday and Saturday from 4:30pm the rest of the year. ◎ *Map C3*

3 Les Olivades, Avignon
The company has been producing and printing Provençal fabrics since 1818. It's now the only such outfit in the region, with materials, table linen and wedding gowns. ◎ *28 rue des Marchands • Map B3*

4 Chocolaterie Castelain, Châteauneuf-du-Pape
An unpromising looking warehouse, but the chocolate wizardry within is dazzling. Enter only if you have iron self-control. ◎ *Rte de Sorgues • Map B3*

5 Les Délices du Luberon, L'Isle-sur-la-Sorgue
Another warehouse and full, this time, of olives, olive preparations and olive derivatives such as tapenade or *melet* (fennel, peppers, olives and anchovies). ◎ *270 ave Voltaire • Map C3*

6 Edith Mézard, Notre-Dame-des-Lumières
The little chateau near Goult provides a perfect setting for beautifully embroidered clothes and a great range of linen for the house. ◎ *Château de l'Ange • Map C3*

7 Confiserie Artisanale Denis Ceccon, Apt
Apt is the proud world capital of crystallized fruit, and Denis Ceccon is one of the few remaining artisans to work by traditional methods – try his apricots. ◎ *24 quai de la Liberté • Map C3*

8 Linda Lorentz, St Martin de Castillon
Californian Linda Lorentz is one of Provence's best goat's cheese producers. Find her by snaking up the road from the village towards Viens, or at Apt's market. ◎ *Hautes Courennes • Map C3*

9 Silvain Frères, St Didier
This is a farming and fruit-growing family also known for their own delicious nougat. There's honey to be had here, as well. ◎ *Map C3*

10 Château Pasquié, Mormoiron
The chateau has lovely grounds and first-rate Mont Ventoux wines. ◎ *Rte de Flassan • Map C2*

Around Provence – Vaucluse

Price Categories

For a three-course meal for one with half a bottle of wine (or equivalent meal), taxes and extra charges.

€	under €30
€€	€30–40
€€€	€40–50
€€€€	€50–60
€€€€€	over €60

Above **La Mirande, Avignon**

🔟 Places to Eat

1 Le Moulin de Lourmarin, Lourmarin
Chef Edouard Loubet is known for aromatic Provençale cuisine – he picks his own herbs to accompany dishes such as roast wild pigeon *(see p50)*. ✆ *Rue du Temple • Map C3 • 04 90 68 06 69 • DA • €€€€€*

2 La Mirande, Avignon
Fine eating in historical splendour right by the Papal Palace. Try the mullet grilled with thyme, calamari, peppers and sweet onions. Summer dining is on the terrace looking on to the palace *(see p51)*. ✆ *Pl La Mirande • Map B3 • 04 90 85 93 93 • DA • €€€€€*

3 Christian Etienne, Avignon
Also next door to the palace, Etienne has frescoes, a terrace and a way with Provençale fare – notably truffles and tomatoes. ✆ *10 rue de Mons • Map B3 • 04 90 86 16 50 • Closed Sun–Mon • €€€€€*

4 Auberge de la Fenière, Lourmarin
One of France's rare female top chefs brings international influence to regional cuisine. ✆ *Rte de Cadenet • Map C3 • 04 90 68 11 79 • Closed Mon, Tue L, Dec–Jan • DA • €€€€*

5 Auberge du Beaucet, Le Beaucet
The hamlet is remote but the refined Provençale cooking is a treat – try rabbit with morel mushrooms. Booking essential. ✆ *Map C3 • 04 90 66 10 82 • Closed Sun–Mon, Dec–Jan • €€*

6 Table du Comtat, Séguret
Old stone elegance and the artistry of Frank Gomez, with dishes such as pigeon with figs, and a bottle from nearby Gigondas *(see p53)*. ✆ *Village centre • Map C3 • 04 90 46 91 49 • Closed Sun D (Oct–Mar), Tue D, Wed (Oct–Jun) • DA • €€€*

7 Hiely Lucullus, Avignon
One of Avignon's oldest restaurants, yet with a lightness of touch to its classic dishes. ✆ *5 rue de la République • Map B3 • 04 90 86 17 07 • Closed Tue–Wed (Sep–Jun) • €€*

8 La Fête en Provence, Vaison-la-Romaine
Surrounded by medieval walls and lovely gardens, the terrace is a great spot to appreciate the occasionally organic cuisine. How about warm pâté with olives and wine sauce? ✆ *Pl du Marché • Map C2 • 04 90 36 36 43 • Closed Wed, mid-Nov–mid-Mar • €€*

9 Moulin à Huile, Vaison-la-Romaine
Superb setting in the medieval part of town. The excellent Provençale cooking is of a standard to match. ✆ *1 quai du Maréchal Foch • Map C2 • 04 90 36 20 67 • Closed Sun D, Mon • €€€€€*

🔟 La Fourchette, Avignon
Much favoured by Avignon folk for its country inn style and treatment of Provençale classics, like *bœuf en daube (see p51)*. ✆ *17 rue Racine • Map B3 • 04 90 85 20 93 • Closed Sat–Sun • €*

Note: *Unless otherwise stated, all restaurants accept credit cards and serve vegetarian meals*

125

STREETSMART

PROVENCE'S TOP 10

Left **Nice Côte d'Azur airport** Right **Provençal motorway**

🔟 Getting to Provence

1 Flying to Nice

Nice Côte d'Azur Airport is the best gateway for Nice, eastern Provence and the Cote d'Azur and Monaco, with frequent flights from Paris, London, New York and other major cities. Flight times are around two hours from the UK, one hour from Paris and nine from New York. The airport is 7 km (4.5 miles) west of Nice and 17 km (10.5 miles) west of Antibes. Buses to Nice bus and railway stations run every 10 minutes. A taxi to the centre costs around €20. There are hourly buses to Antibes and Cannes, and buses every 90 minutes to Monaco, 45 minutes away. Most international flights use the east terminal; domestic flights use the west terminal.
🔊 *Airport information: 08 20 42 33 33.*

2 Flying to Marseille

Marignane (Marseille-Provence) Airport is handy for central Provence, Aix, Avignon and Marseille itself. The airport is 25 km (17 miles) northwest of the city centre and 24 km (15 miles) southeast of Aix. Buses run to Marseille-St Charles railway station every 20 minutes. Taxis to the centre cost around €40. International flights use both terminals.
🔊 *Airport information: 04 42 14 14 14*

3 Flying to Nîmes

Nîmes, just beyond Provence's western border, is the landing place for cheap charter flights and is a good gateway for Provence, particularly the Camargue, Bouches-du-Rhône, Arles or Avignon. The airport is 8 km (5 miles) southeast of the city with buses every 30 minutes. Taxis into Nîmes cost around €20.
🔊 *Airport information: 04 66 70 06 88*

4 Fly-drive

Packages which involve a flight and a hire car, available from airlines and tour operators, can be cheaper than taking your own car. However, main car rental companies have desks at Marseille and Nice airports and offices in major towns including Avignon, Nice, Cannes, Marseille, Monaco and St-Tropez.

5 Using the Internet

International and specialist airline, ferry and rail websites are worth checking out before you go – flying, for instance, can often be cheaper than going by rail, and driving is usually the most expensive option.

6 By Train

The new TGV Méditerranée high-speed train takes just three hours to travel between Paris and Marseille, with stops at Avignon and Aix. Journey time to Marseille from London is under seven hours, including a change from the sub-Channel Eurostar service to TGV in Lille.

7 Motorail

French Railways (SNCF) operate a seasonal overnight motorail service from Calais to Avignon and Nice, transporting cars while their owners travel in sleeping compartments.

8 By Road

Avignon, gateway to Provence by road, is around 1,000 km (640 miles) from the Channel ports. The fastest drive, via France's Autoroute du Soleil, takes around 8.5 hours and costs around €50 in tolls. Avoiding toll motorways *(péages)* lengthens the journey time by six hours.

9 By River

The most romantic and stress-free way to arrive in Provence is on a Rhône river cruiser. Many cruise lines operate luxury, full-board river cruises between Lyon and Avignon.

10 Celebrity-style

Chartering a jet to fly, as the stars do, direct into Cannes airport (used only by private aircraft) may break your budget, but helicopter flights from Nice to Monaco and Cannes are quite affordable and an exciting way to start your holiday.

Above **Boats moored in St-Tropez**

Getting Around Provence

1 Car Rental
Renting a car on arrival can be cheaper than driving your own car. Other advantages include left-hand drive and replacement vehicles if the one you rent breaks down. Packages combining flights, car rental and accommodation can be very good value, or you can rent a vehicle for part of your stay from major rental companies at airports or in all main towns and resorts. Most car rental companies require drivers to be over 21 with a clean record.

2 By car
If travelling from elsewhere in Europe, using your own car has its advantages: you can bring more luggage, see more of France, and take home more souvenirs. You must have adequate insurance cover and French law also requires modifications to headlights and a range of accessories including fire extinguisher, replacement bulb set, warning triangle and first-aid kit. Emergency breakdown insurance is also advisable: consult your insurer or motoring organization.

3 Taxis
Taxis are reliable and use meters *(compteurs)* but are not flagged down on the street – find one at a taxi rank, book by phone, or ask your hotel or restaurant to call one.

4 City Transport
France has some of the best public transport in Europe and getting around the region's major cities by bus, tram and (in Marseille) metro presents few problems. Fares are integrated, so a single ticket can be used on any combination of transport for one hour. Day passes and books of tickets *(carnets)* are also available *(see p135)*.

5 By Train
From Marseille, rail lines run west to Arles and Nîmes, north to Aix and Avignon and east to Nice and Monaco. TER (regional express trains) also operate an inland route from Nice to Digne-les-Bains. A range of discounts is available *(see p135)*.

6 Inter-city Bus
Inter-city buses supplement trains between major cities and numerous companies operating from long-distance bus stations *(gares routières)* in cities and larger towns. Smaller villages and rural towns are poorly served by buses: many villages have no service at all, others have only one or two services a day.

7 Cycle Routes
Cycling is a great way to explore Provence. Mountainous regions such as the Vaucluse and the Alpes may be only for the super-fit, but

there are gentler rides in the lowlands, along the coast and in the dead-flat Camargue. Mountain bikes *(velos tous terrains or VTT)* can be hired in all major towns and resorts (tourist offices have lists) and marked cycle trails range from demanding to totally relaxed *(see p57)*.

8 Walking Trails
Provence is superb walking country, offering guided or marked walks through historic cities and coastal paths, *sentiers balisés* (local trails) and *sentiers de grande randonnée* (long-distance hiking tracks), part of a network that crosses France. Main long distance trails are the GR5, GR51 GR6 and GR9. Maps and guides are available from tourist offices *(see p57)*.

9 On Horseback
Horses can be hired by the day or for longer, with or without a guide, on gentle or more demanding trails. The Camargue especially is ideal riding country *(see pp20–21)*.

10 Yachts and Cruisers
The Riviera is prime sailing country and every kind of vessel, from small yachts and catamarans to fully crewed motor-cruisers, can be chartered out of marinas including Nice, Cannes, St-Tropez, Antibes and St-Jean.

Above **Provençal tourist office**

📖10 Sources of Information

1 Tourist Offices

Information on sights, events, travel and places to stay is available from many sources including the French national tourist office (with offices abroad), regional and city tourist offices and, in villages, the local *Syndicat d'Initiative*. You'll also find information desks at airports and main railway stations *(see p128)*. Staff are multilingual and guides and maps are available in English and other major European languages.

2 Government Tourist Offices

The French Government Tourist Office (Maison de la France) is a one-stop shop for information on how to get to Provence, what to see and where to stay *(see box)*.

3 Comité Régional du Tourisme

The Regional Committee for Tourism for Provence-Alpes-Côte d'Azur is based in Marseille, with multilingual maps, guides and a hotel finding and booking service. The tourist office of the Bouches-du-Rhône is also based in Marseille and has a handy website. 🖎 *Comité Departementale du Tourisme Provence-Alpes-Côte d'Azur: 14 rue Ste-Barbe, Marseille, map C5, 04 93 32 24 94 • CDT Bouches-du-Rhône: 13 rue Roux de Brignoles, Marseille, 04 91 13 84 13, www.visitprovence.com*

4 Cannes Tourist Office

The main information source for Cannes and the Côte d'Azur is in the town centre. It has a website to help you plan your trip, multilingual guides and maps and information on nightlife and events. 🖎 *Palais des Festivals, La Croisette BP 272, Cannes • Map G4 • 04 93 39 24 53 • www.cannes-on-line.com*

5 Nice Tourist Office

This should be your first stop in town for maps, guides, help with finding accommodation, and information on what's on in Nice. 🖎 *1 esplanade Kennedy, BP 4079 Nice • Map H4 • 04 93 92 82 82 • www.nicetourism.com*

6 Alpes-Maritimes Tourist Office

For information on where to stay, where to go and what to do in Nice's hinterland contact the Communalité Regionale du Tourisme, also located in Nice. 🖎 *55 promenade des Anglais, Nice • Map H4 • 04 93 37 78 78*

7 Monaco Tourist Office

Practical information on all aspects of travel in the area is available from the Monaco Direction du Tourisme de la Principauté de Monaco. 🖎 *2a blvd des Moulins, Monte Carlo • Map H4 • 00 377 92 166 166 • www.monaco-congres.com*

8 Alpes-de-Haute-Provence Tourist Office

For information on events, transport and hotels in the Alpes-de-Haute-Provence. 🖎 *19 rue Dr Honnorat, Digne-les-Bains • Map E2 • 04 92 31 57 29*

9 Var Tourist Office

The main information source for the Var region. 🖎 *1 blvd Foch, BP 99, Draguignan • Map F4 • 04 94 50 55 50*

10 Vaucluse Tourist Office

The Vaucluse office is Avignon-based and also has a useful website. 🖎 *12 rue Collège de la Croix, BP 147, Avignon • Map B3 • 04 90 80 47 00 • www.provenceguide.com*

French Government Tourist Offices

Australia
25 Bligh St, Level 22, Sydney NSW 2000 • 02 9231 5244

France
127 ave des Champs-Elysées, 75008 Paris • 08 36 68 31 12

United Kingdom
178 Piccadilly, London W1V 0AL • 09068 244123 • www.franceguide.com

USA
444 Madison Ave, New York, NY 10022 • 212 838 7800

ATTENTION AU FEU

Left **August crowds** Right **Forest fire warning sign**

TOP 10 Things to Avoid

1 Autoroutes in August
French *autoroutes* (motorways) are very crowded in August, especially during the first and last weekends of the month, when huge numbers of holiday-makers from northern France head at top speed for the sunny south. There are long traffic jams and often serious accidents. Avoid driving south at these times if possible.

2 Cannes Film Festival
For two weeks in May it becomes impossible to find a hotel room or a table at a good restaurant in Cannes as the resort is overrun with up to 30,000 film stars and their entourages, directors, producers, financiers, journalists and other hangers-on. This is strictly an insider's event, and unless you have Hollywood ambitions, give Cannes a wide berth during the festival (see p58).

3 Monte Carlo Rally and Monaco Grand Prix
Monaco is host to two of the world's most prestigious motor sports events, the Rallye Monte Carlo every January and the Monaco Grand Prix, at differing dates during the Grand Prix season (see p59). Both are worth avoiding – it's claimed that to be sure of a room during either event it is

necessary to book 10 years ahead. Both events take place through the city streets, so much of Monaco is closed off.

4 Bullfights
The traditional Provençal bullfight (course à la cocarde) is a bloodless affair in which the bullfighter (razeteur) tries to snatch a red ribbon (cocarde) from the horns of an increasingly irritated bull. In the arenas of Arles and Nîmes, however, Spanish-style corridas, in which the bull is tormented and then killed, are often part of the entertainment. These are advertised as mise à mort (to the death)

5 Motoring Offences
Police issue heavy fines on the spot for speeding and for other motoring offences. The blood alcohol limit for drink-driving is low: one glass of wine or a 33cl bottle of beer will take you close to the limit, two will exceed it. Drivers who cannot pay fines in cash on the spot have their vehicles impounded.

6 Dangerous Drivers
After Greece and Portugal, France has the worst road accident record in the EU. Many French motorists drive aggressively, overtake carelessly and ignore safe braking distances on motorways. Expect the unexpected at all times.

7 Hotel Telephones
Many hotels charge very high rates for international phone calls. It is far cheaper to call from a post office or telephone booth using coins, a credit card or phonecard (see p138).

8 Cheap Wine
With the cheapest vins de pays (local wines) costing as little as €4.00 for a five-litre plastic flagon, there is a strong temptation to look no further. Many of these wines are quite drinkable but some are guaranteed to produce a crippling hangover. For a few euros more, France has far better wines to offer.

9 Lighting Fires
The South of France has a serious forest fire problem in July and August, when undergrowth and pine forests are tinder dry. High risk areas are closed from the beginning of July to mid-September, and lighting camp fires anywhere in the region is strictly forbidden.

10 Hurrying
It takes a little time to adapt to the relaxed pace of Provence, but there is little point in rushing things. Almost everything closes for lunch between noon and 3pm. As the Provençal proverb goes: "Slow in the mornings, and not too fast in the afternoons."

Left **Gites de France logo** Centre **Typical chateau hotel** Right **Hotel doorman**

TOP 10 Accommodation Tips

1 High and Low Season

Don't even think about visiting Provence in high season without reserving accommodation. From the beginning of July to the end of August the region, especially the Riviera and Côte d'Azur, is at its busiest and everything, from grand hotels to campsites, is full. May to mid-June and September to mid-October are less crowded. Some smaller hotels in rural areas close from November to February.

2 How to Book

You can book direct with hotels and other accommodation providers by phone, fax and, increasingly, by email and via the web. The site www.franceguide.com provides useful links to sites where you can find and book accommodation. You will normally be asked for a deposit, which you can pay by credit card in most larger hotels and campsites, or by money order.

3 Families

The South of France is very well geared up for family tourism, both on the coast and inland. Many hotels will provide an extra bed for smaller children or a cot for babies at a nominal cost. *Gites (see p147)* and camp sites *(see p144)* also offer excellent value for families travelling on

a budget. Most camp sites have facilities and activities for children.

4 On a Budget

The best way to save money is to travel off-season (and avoid the glitzy Riviera resorts). However, accommodation in France can be surprisingly cheap, with rooms in small *pensions* available for as little as €30 for a double room *(see p145)*. Hotels in Maison de la France's *Bon Weekend en Villes* programme *(see p130)* offer two nights for the price of one at hotels in towns including Aix, Arles, Avignon and Marseille.

5 Camping

Camp sites in Provence usually feature pools, playgrounds, café-bar and often a mini-market and morning bread delivery. They become crowded in July and August, and most close their gates by 10pm. Independent camping is discouraged, as is sleeping on beaches.

6 Hotel Chains

France pioneered the "limited service hotel" which offers clean, comfortable rooms at budget prices, and not much else. Chains such as Formule 1, Campanile, Etap and others cluster at motorway junctions, airports and on the out-skirts of cities. Although lacking in character they

can be perfect for the first and last night of your stay.

7 Self-catering

Accommodation in *gites* is plentiful – most are privately owned and often in pretty cottages or farmhouses. Crockery and kitchen utensils are supplied, but you usually have to bring your own bedlinen and do your own cleaning.

8 Villas

A villa holiday offers a more luxurious version of self-catering. Most villas are in or near coastal resorts and usually have a pool. They offer basic maid service (cleaning and linen change) but the more luxurious can be fully staffed with cook, valet service and chauffeur.

9 Apartments

Holiday apartments can be found in most resort areas, especially in the Cannes-Antibes area, but few offer the facilities of a *gite* or villa and most are geared to long stays.

10 Yachts and Cruisers

You don't have to be mega-rich to stay on a yacht or cruiser. The closer you get to Cannes or Antibes the more expensive such boats become, but there are less ostentatious vessels in such harbours as Le Lavandou and Ste-Maxime.

Left **Provence fruit market** Centre **Fresh salad** Right **Pavement café**

TOP 10 Eating and Drinking Tips

1 Cafés and Bars

There's not much to choose in Provence between establishments calling themselves cafés and those which call themselves bars. All serve alcoholic drinks and coffee all day, and most serve simple snacks such as ham, cheese or salami sandwiches. Village cafés usually close around 8pm but city and resort café-bars stay open much later, some until dawn.

2 Menus

Most restaurants have several set menus, the cheapest usually starting as low as €7.00. If you are not sure what to order, these menus are excellent value. Eating à la carte (selecting each dish yourself) is usually more expensive.

3 Pichet and Pression

Wine served by the *pichet* (jug) – usually the local *vin de pays*, bought by the barrel and decanted – is usually much cheaper than wine by the glass or bottle, and always palatable. If you want a draught beer, ask for a *une pression*; if you order *"une bière"* you will be served a more expensive, bottled beer.

4 Picnics

The Provençaux, like all French people, love picnics, and when you plan an *al fresco* lunch at the beach or in the country you will be spoilt for choice. *Boulangeries* (bakeries) and *pâtisseries* (pastry shops) sell a wonderful choice of loaves, rolls and pastries and most *patisseries* sell delicious ready-made sandwiches. Provence's typical takeaway snack is the *pan bagnat*, a crusty roll soaked in olive oil and stuffed with *salade Niçoise (see p51)*. To make your own sandwiches, head for the village *traiteur*, *charcuterie* or supermarket to buy cuts of cold meats, chicken and sausage.

5 Vegetarians

Vegetarians are poorly served in Provençal restaurants. Few offer anything more than salad, omelette or cheese – soups almost always contain meat stock. However, vegetarians catering for themselves will find mouthwatering fresh fruit and vegetables, delicious cheeses, Provençal ingredients such as truffles, olives, pine nuts and garlic and dozens of aromatic herbs.

6 Wine "en vrac"

Throughout Provence signs invite the traveller to visit local wineries (*caves cooperatives*) and enjoy a tasting (*dégustation*), after which you will be expected to buy at least a bottle. If staying in self-catering accommodation, this is a good opportunity to invest in a *vrac* (plastic barrel) containing five or ten litres of wine, usually at competitive prices.

7 Water

Water as well as wine is always drunk with meals and even in up-market restaurants it's accepted to ask for a *carafe d'eau* (jug of tap water) rather than a bottle of mineral water.

8 Soft Drinks

Soft drinks are no cheaper than wine or beer. Typical Provençal offerings include a range of sweet cordials with ice and water: mint syrup (*syrop de menthe*), blackcurrant (*cassis*), grenadine and tart lemon juice (*citron pressé*).

9 Bloody, Rare or Well-done

If you like your steak well done, order it *"bien cuit"*. If you prefer it very rare, ask for *"saignant"* (literally, "bleeding") and if you like your steak barely cooked ask for *"bleu"* (blue).

10 Bills and Tipping

In cafés the bill for each drink is brought to your table with your order but there is no need to pay until you leave. A small tip is customary. In restaurants, menu prices normally include the tip, but an extra five to ten per cent gratuity for good service is expected.

For gourmet restaurants in Provence **See pp50–51**

Left **Bags of dried herbs** Right **Provençal olive seller**

Shopping Tips

1 Tax and Allowances

If you live within the EU you can take home as much wine, spirits, tobacco and perfume as you wish, although if you are travelling by air you are unlikely to be able to find room in your weight allowance for more than two bottles of wine or spirits. If you live outside the EU you are limited to two bottles. Non-EU residents can claim back the value added tax (TVA) included in the sales price on purchases worth more than €180 in one shop, to be exported within three months.

2 Wine

For wine to take home, the world-class appellations of the Côtes du Rhône, and especially those of Châteauneuf-du-Pape *(see p53)*, are the best investment. You can buy them young to drink straight away, or let them age for up to seven years for a long-lasting souvenir.

3 Herbs

Bunches of oregano and thyme can be bought in markets or in packaged form in supermarkets – they will add the scents and flavours of the south to your kitchen long after you reach home. They make attractive gifts too, as do bags of dried lavender packed in local fabrics, but check your home country's rules on importing foodstuffs.

4 Truffles

Truffles must be the ultimate high-value, low-weight souvenir or gift to take home. Taking up next to no space in your luggage, the "black diamonds" from the Vaucluse cost as much as €180 per kilogram, so there's no risk of buying too many. Best places to buy include Puyméras, Richerenches and Valréas, all in the Vaucluse region *(see p51)*.

5 Olives, Olive Oil and Olivewood

Nothing, perhaps, is more typical of Provence than the olive tree and its fruit. For happy memories of meals in the sun, take home virgin olive oil – the best is said to come from around Nyons, in the Vaucluse, or from the Vallée de la Baux olive groves of the Alpilles region. Or you could buy a jar of green olives with Provençal herbs, bars of savon de Marseille olive oil soap, or attractive, practical salad bowls, forks and salad spoons carved from close-grained olivewood.

6 Cheese

The French gift for presentation makes local produce irresistible (as it's intended to). Make one last visit to a market or *épicier* (grocer) to fill your basket with goat's cheese wrapped in chestnut leaves or numerous other fabulous options.

7 Santon Figures

Santons ("little saints") were originally designed to decorate Nativity scenes at Christmas but these pottery figures make unique Provençal mementos and gifts. There are dozens of different figures, each representing a traditional trade or skill. They can be found all over the region, but are especially popular in Marseille.

8 Perfume

Perfumed oils, lavender water or orange water, and bubble baths and shampoos scented with different fragrances can be found on the shelves of Provence's many fine perfumiers.

9 Museum Prints

Museum-quality reproductions of works by the masters who have lived in Provence *(see pp36–7)* are on sale at gallery shops attached to the region's leading museums of art *(see pp34–5)*. Weighing very little and rolling up into a conveniently small package, unframed prints are excellent purchases to take home.

10 Confectionery

As gifts, Provençal confectionery such as *calissons*, the almond-paste sweetmeats from Aix, are perfect, as are *marrons glacés*, and preserved lemons, figs and other fruits.

Left **Museum cards** Right **Student ID card**

🔟 Provence on a Budget

1 Off-season Travel
During July and August, when Provence throngs with thousands of French and foreign holidaymakers, the price of everything, from a beach deckchair to a hotel room, is highest. Provence is much cheaper (and pleasanter) in May and June and in September and October.

2 Carnets
Buying a *carnet* of five or ten tickets from bus and railway stations for public transport in larger towns such as Marseille, Nice and Monaco is cheaper and more convenient than buying single tickets.

3 Discounts
Many museums and attractions offer discounted admission to students and professionals such as teachers and journalists. Proof of status, such as a college or university ID card, press card or teacher ID card, is required.

4 Rail Passes
French Railways (SNCF) offer the France Railpass, which is hard to beat for flexibility and value for money. It allows from three to nine days travel on any route, from high-speed TGVs *(see p129)* to mountain railways, anywhere in France within one month. The Senior France Railpass for people over 60 is valid for groups of up to eight

and for first-class travel. Both passes are available at all major French railway stations, but for convenience can also be booked via travel agents before you leave home.

5 Youth Hostels
Youth hostels can be found in Marseille, Nice, Menton, St-Raphaël, Aix and Arles, and at several national parks. Despite the name, there is no age limit for travellers. For more information contact the Fédération Unie des Auberges de Jeunesse (FUAJ) in Paris.
⚫ *FUAJ: 01 44 89 87 27*

6 No-Frills Airlines
The British-based "no-frills" airlines sell their best fares on their websites. Those flying to Provence from the UK include Ryanair to Nîmes, easyJet and Go! to Nice, and Buzz to Marseille.
⚫ *Ryanair: www.ryanair. com • easyJet: www. easyjet.com • Go: www. gofly.com • Buzz: www. buzzaway.com*

7 Museum Cards
Multi-site and multiple entry passes for sights and museums include the *Carte Musée Côte d'Azur*, allowing unlimited access to more than 50 museums, sold through local tourist offices *(see p130)* and at museums. A three-day pass costs €10, a seven-day pass €20. *La Clef des Temps* (Key to Time)

costs €15 from tourist offices and allows entry to 10 historic monuments throughout the Provence and Côte d'Azur region.

8 Camping
Provençal camp sites can be quite lavish affairs, with swimming pools, self-service laundry, mini-market and restaurant and are good value, but are not always cheaper than simple hotels *(see p144)*.

9 Working Holidays
Grape-picking is hard work and although pickers *(vendangeurs)* usually receive lunch and dinner daily as well as their pay, accommodation is not always part of the deal. The *vendange* (harvest) in Provence is from mid-September to mid-October. Recruiting starts as early as May, and the best way to find work is to call or write directly to as many *domaines* (estates) as possible. Lists of wine growers who recruit foreign workers are available from local tourist offices.

🔟 Hitch-hiking
Hitch-hiking is permitted on all roads except *autoroutes* (motorways), and in some rural areas is the only cheap alternative to infrequent village buses. Use caution: women are advised not to hitch-hike solo and travel after dark is also not advisable.

For value for money accommodation **See p145**

135

Left **Camp site accommodation** Right **Provence beach**

Tips for Families

1 Hotels
Young children can usually share a room with parents at no extra cost. Hotels such as those in the Campanile and Formule 1 chains *(see p132)*, located at motorway junctions and near major towns and airports, offer family rooms which sleep three to five people for the same price as for two. Many youth hostels also have comfortable family rooms which are ideal for families with older children *(see p135)*.

2 Camp Sites
Camp sites in Provence are very much geared to cater for families, with play areas for children and large discounts for under 12s. Some more expensive camp sites also offer supervised activities for children *(see p145)*.

3 Children's Menus
Children are welcome in almost all restaurants and are not excluded from cafés and bars. Restaurants do not usually provide special facilities for children such as high chairs. Some, especially those in tourist resorts, offer fixed-price menus for children, at around half the price.

4 Activities
Many resorts on the coast, as well as national and regional parks, offer a range of organized activities and events for children during the summer season. A schedule of events is usually available from the local tourist office, to be found even in very small villages *(see p130)*. Many French festival events *(see pp58–9)* culminate in fireworks displays which will delight older children but may terrify toddlers. Children will also enjoy the sound and light shows held throughout the summer season at many castles and other historic buildings.

5 Public Transport
Children are eligible for free or reduced price travel on French Railways (SNCF) trains and buses and on urban public transport. Babies normally travel free.

6 Car Rental
Use of child safety seats and rear seat belts is obligatory under French law. All major car rental companies will provide children's safety seats if requested in advance. There is normally a small charge for this service.

7 On the Beach
Most beaches along the Côte d'Azur and the Riviera are safe for children, with shallow waters, gentle waves and lifeguards on duty in many places. However, sensible precautions should be taken. Babies, toddlers and older children are at risk of sunburn from April to October, and use of high-factor, waterproof sun block is advisable. Beaches become very crowded during July and August, making it easy for toddlers to become separated from parents. On rocky beaches, look out for black sea urchins with spines which give painful stings.

8 Self-catering
Using self-catering accommodation gives parents greater flexibility and allows families to keep to the mealtimes and bedtimes they are accustomed to instead of living by hotel schedules.

9 Motorway Services
French *autoroute* service areas cater very well for parents with babies and small children, with clean, spacious nappy (diaper) changing areas, toddlers' toilets, disposable nappy (diaper) vending machines and baby food on sale in service area shops.

10 Nappies (Diapers) and other Necessities
Remember that French opening hours are much more restrictive than those in the UK *(see p134)*. Parents should make sure they have stocks of necessities to last through the long French weekend.

Left **Wheelchair ramp** Right **Outside restaurant tables**

🔟 Tips for Disabled Travellers

1 Before You Leave
RADAR (the Royal Association for Disability and Rehabilitation) provides information to help disabled and older people travel abroad. Holiday Care, the UK's central source of travel and holiday information for disabled people, has information sheets on accessible accommodation and attractions in France. The website www.faa.gov/acr/dat.htm outlines airline rules for access and seating for wheelchair users and other people with disabilities on scheduled and charter flights. *◈ RADAR: 12 City Forum, 250 City Rd, London EC1V 8AF, 020 7250 3222, www.radar.org. uk • Holiday Care: holiday. care@virgin.net*

2 Holiday Companies
Access Travel offers wheelchair-accessible properties which have been personally inspected or suggested by a wheelchair-user. They also offer special air fares worldwide and will liaise with airlines to arrange special services. The travel website www. youreable.com offers advice on organizing your holiday, insurance, passports, health, online accommodation guides and specialized holidays for people with all types of disabilities. *◈ Access Travel: www.access-travel.co.uk*

3 Airports
Assistance for wheel-chair users and other disabilities is offered at Nice airport by Service Handicapés. A similar service is operated at Marseille airport by the Société d'Assistance Midi-Provence. *◈ Service Handicapés GIS: 04 93 21 44 58 • Societé d'Assistance Midi-Provence: 04 42 14 27 42*

4 Museums and Galleries
Admission is free to blind people and others in need of assistance in most major museums and art galleries in Nice, Avignon and Marseille. Most also have audio guides in English and French. Some also have braille guides.

5 Public Transport
Free or reduced rate transport is available in Nice and Marseille for people with disabilities and their carers. SNCF French Railways has an accessibility helpline. For wheelchair access to trains, book in advance. SOS Voyageurs also offers help to older travellers. *◈ SNCF helpline: 0800 15 47 53 • SOS Voyageurs: 04 93 82 62 11 (Nice); 04 91 62 12 80 (Marseille)*

6 Accommodation
Most mid-priced 2- to 3-star hotels have elevators. Many motel-style hotel chains have wheel-chair access direct from the car park. Gîtes de France publishes a guide to accessible farmhouse accommodation available through Maison de la France *(see p130)*. The Association des Paralysés de France publishes a guide to accessible accommodation (in French) titled *Où Ferons-Nous Etape? (Where Can We Stay?)*. *◈ Association des Paralysés de France: 17 blvd August Blanqui, 75013 Paris, 01 40 78 69 00*

7 Restaurants
Most restaurants have poor access for wheel-chair users. In summer, picking an outside table eases the problem.

8 Loisirs Provence Mediterranée
This company organizes holidays in Provence for people with disabilities, mainly in gîtes. *◈ Loisirs Provence Mediterranée: 36 rue St-Jacques, 13006 Marseille, 04 91 04 20 20, lpm@lpm.asso.fr*

9 SCOP
The association for people with cerebral palsy publishes a guide to wheelchair accessible accommodation, transport and museums throughout France (in French). *◈ SCOP, 4 rue Gustave-Rouanet, 75018 Paris, 01 42 52 97 00*

10 Minitel
Minitel *(see p138)* has an information section for people with disabilities.

NE LAISSEZ PAS UN RHUME VOUS GACHER LA VIE !

Télécarte 50

LA POSTE

Left **French phonecard** Right **Postbox**

TOP10 Banking and Communication

1 Language and Etiquette

English is widely spoken by people working in coastal resorts, tourist offices, hotels, larger restaurants and airports. It is less fluently spoken in urban Marseille and in rural communities, where you will need a grasp of French in order to understand and be understood. Etiquette is highly valued: shake hands on being introduced and use the titles *"Monsieur"* and *"Madame"* on greeting.

2 Changing Money

Foreign currency and travellers' cheques in all major currencies can be changed into euros at exchange offices and banks. French francs ceased to be legal tender in February 2002. Euro notes are issued in denominations of €5, €10, €20, €50, €100, €200 and €500 and coins in 2-euro, 1-euro, and 50, 20, 10, 5, 2 and 1 euro cents. The euro is legal tender in 12 European countries. Cash and travellers' cheques can be changed at larger post offices. Banks are usually open 9am– noon and 2–5pm Monday to Friday, but some also open on Saturday. You can also change money at larger hotels.

3 Credit and Debit Cards

Cash can be drawn from your bank or credit card account using automatic teller machines (ATMs) in all towns and larger villages. On-screen instructions are in English and French. Credit cards can be used to pay for motorway tolls but smaller shops, restaurants, hotels, camp sites and *gîte* operators prefer cash.

4 Public Phones

International and local calls can be made from telephone booths even in the smallest communities, with cards or euro coins. Some phones accept only French telephone debit cards *(télécartes)* which can be bought from post offices, newsagents and *tabacs* (tobacconists) in denominations of 50 and 120 units. You can also call from metered telephone booths at large post offices, or via the *pays direct* service which allows you to place your call through an operator in your home country and pay by credit card, charge card, or reversing the charges. The code for the UK is 00 44, followed by the local code (omitting the zero) and number. For Canada and the USA the code is 01; Australia, 61; and New Zealand, 64.

5 Mobile Phones

Reception is generally good but it may be hard to obtain a signal in deep mountain valleys. Better reception can be obtained by heading for higher ground.

6 Post Offices

Most post offices open 9am–noon and 2–5pm Monday to Friday and 9am–noon on Saturday. Stamps are sold singly or in books of ten *(carnets)* and are also sold in *tabacs*.

7 Fax and Poste Restante

Faxes can be sent or received at any post office. For a small fee you can also use the *poste restante* service to receive mail at any post office. Letters must be addressed using the five-digit postal code and surname before forename.

8 Internet

There are internet cafés in all main towns, larger villages and most coastal resorts.

9 Minitel

A telescreen information system installed in post offices and some hotels. It offers a range of services including railway timetables, telephone numbers and addresses for companies throughout France.

10 Newspapers

The English-language *International Herald Tribune* is published daily in Paris and available in resorts and at station newsagents in big cities on day of publication. British daily papers usually arrive in resorts the day after publication.

Left **Ambulance** Right **Sunbathers protected by sunscreen**

🔟 Security and Health

1 Emergencies
Service d'Aide Médicale Urgence, the 24-hour emergency medical service, can send an ambulance, paramedic or a doctor. For most emergencies payment in cash is required immediately after treatment. ✆ *Service d'Aide Médicale Urgence: 01 47 07 77 77*

2 Travel Insurance
France has excellent health care but treatment is not free. Take out adequate insurance to cover all emergencies – policies are available through your credit card company, bank, motoring association, household insurance company, or direct from insurers. Policies sold by travel agents are more expensive. For citizens of EU countries, form E111, available from post offices before you leave home, entitles visitors to free health care but only for basic treatment. Instructions are on the form.

3 Minor Ailments
Provence has no serious health risks. Tap water is safe, but water from village fountains should be drunk only if it bears the sign *"eau potable"*. Sunburn is a risk throughout the summer: wear a hat and sunscreen. In early summer hay fever sufferers should carry antihistamine tablets or drops. Change of diet and climate can cause diarrhoea or indigestion. Remedies are available from pharmacies.

4 Insects and Pests
Mosquitoes are common in summer. Repellents containing deet (diethyltoluamide) and/or citronella oil will keep them away. Plug-in electric repellent pads which keep bedrooms mosquito-free can be bought at pharmacies. On rocky beaches, beware of treading on spiky sea urchins; when swimming, watch out for stinging jellyfish. Hornets and scorpions, both of which have a painful but non-lethal sting, are harmless unless provoked. You will encounter snakes on country walks, but the only venomous species, the viper, is shy, rarely seen and harmless unless trodden on.

5 Breakdowns and Accidents
A red warning triangle must be placed 50–100 m (160–300 ft) behind any broken down vehicle. In the event of an accident, call the police/emergency services and await their arrival by your car.

6 Doctors
A 24-hour doctor service (*médécin de garde*) operates in major towns. The telephone number is obtainable from your hotel, telephone operator or pharmacies.

7 Dentists
Dental care services are offered by major hospitals.

8 Hospitals
The accident and emergency clinic (*service des urgences*) of any public hospital will treat injuries and unexpected illnesses. Payment is required immediately.

9 Pharmacies
Pharmacies are indicated by a green cross. French pharmacists are usually helpful in suggesting remedies for minor illnesses. In all towns one pharmacy will open at night and weekends – details are posted on all pharmacy doors.

🔟 Crime
Theft from cars, bags and luggage is prevalent along the Riviera and Côte d'Azur – do not take valuables, passports, tickets or more cash than you need to the beach. Violent crime is less common, but take normal precautions: women should not walk alone late at night, and avoid poorly lit streets and run-down areas.

Emergency Numbers
Police: 17
Ambulance: 15
Fire Brigade: 19

Left **Carlton Inter-Continental, Cannes** Right **Hôtel de Paris, Monte Carlo**

⁑10 Grand Hotels

1 Le Negresco, Nice
The flagship of the whole Riviera, the Negresco is the grandest of grand hotels, from its splendid *belle époque* façade and public areas to its immaculate rooms and attentive service. One of the world's most opulent hotels. ⊗ 37 promenade des Anglais • Map P5 • 04 93 16 64 00 • DA • €€€€€

2 Hôtel du Cap Eden Roc, Antibes
As ostentatious as the Negresco in its way, the Eden Roc is another landmark of the Riviera and has been for more than a century. It offers exclusivity and film-star chic in tropical gardens and is, in a word, idyllic. To keep the hoi polloi out, it accepts no credit cards. ⊗ Blvd Kennedy • Map G4 • 04 93 61 39 01 • edenroc-hotel@wanadoo.fr • No credit cards • DA • €€€€€

3 L'Hermitage, Monte Carlo
The Hermitage recalls the splendour of *belle époque* Monaco, with its glass-domed atrium, its over-the-top restaurant decorated in pink and gold, marble terrace and fine service. A monument in its own right, it is one of Europe's smartest hotels – a reputation it has retained for more than 100 years. ⊗ Sq Beaumarchais • Map H4 • 03 77 92 16 40 00 • hh@sbm.mc • DA • €€€€€

4 Hôtel de Paris, Monte Carlo
Rivaling the Hermitage for *belle époque* splendour, the Hôtel de Paris has a famous café-terrace on the ground floor *(see p102)* and is within staggering distance of the casino *(see pp26–7).* Queen Victoria stayed here, as have a host of other crowned heads and celebrities. ⊗ Pl du Casino • Map H4 • 03 77 92 16 30 00 • DA • €€€€€

5 Carlton Inter-Continental, Cannes
The Carlton is a Cannes landmark, home of the stars during the Film Festival and appropriately luxurious, with its own private beach and high standards of service. Part of an international chain, it retains an individual character. ⊗ 58 La Croisette • Map G4 • 04 93 06 40 25 • cannes@interconti.com • DA • €€€€€

6 Hôtel Metropole, Beaulieu
Yet another relic of the Riviera's aristocratic hey-day, the Metropole is a mock-Renaissance palace with a heated seawater pool, a terrace restaurant with magnificent views, and a more relaxed, less pompous feel than some of the Riviera's other grand hotels. ⊗ 15 blvd Maréchal Leclerc • Map G4 • 04 93 01 00 08 • metropole@relaischateaux.com • DA • €€€€€

7 La Réserve, Beaulieu
Opened in the late 19th century this pink palace in its semi-tropical grounds is a grand place to stay, still retaining the glory of its 1920s heyday. ⊗ 5 blvd Général Leclerc • Map G4 • 04 93 01 00 01 • €€€€€

8 Hôtel Nord-Pinus, Arles
This historic hotel is the best address in Arles. Rooms are comfortable, and the lounge and foyer have a Provençal atmosphere. ⊗ 14 pl du Forum • Map B4 • 04 90 93 44 44 • info@nord-pinus.com • €€€

9 Hôtel d'Arlatan, Arles
Built in the 16th century, this was the town house of the Counts of Arlatan and is steeped in history, with a walled garden and Roman relics in the foyer. ⊗ 26 rue du Sauvage • Map B4 • 04 90 93 56 66 • hotel-arlatan@provnet.fr • No air conditioning • DA • €€€

10 Hôtel de l'Europe, Avignon
Step back in time as you enter the ornate gates of this historic hotel. Heavy wooden furniture and antique tapestries create an elegant atmosphere. ⊗ 12 pl Crillon • Map B3 • 04 90 14 76 76 • reservations@hotel-d-europe.fr • No air conditioning • €€€

Note: *Unless otherwise stated, all hotels accept credit cards, have en-suite bathrooms and air conditioning*

Price Categories

For a standard, double room per night (with breakfast if included), taxes and extra charges.

€	under €100
€€	€100–€150
€€€	€150–€250
€€€€	€250–€350
€€€€€	over €350

Above **Monte Carlo Beach Hotel, Roquebrune-Cap-Martin**

🏅10 Luxury Resorts

1 La Voile d'Or, St-Jean-Cap-Ferrat

This luxury resort hotel next to the quiet (by Riviera standards) port boasts two saltwater pools and a highly regarded restaurant, as well as lush greenery, romantic terraces and excellent service. ◎ *Port de St-Jean • Map G4 • 04 93 01 13 13 • reservation@lavoiledor.fr • €€€€*

2 Martinez, Cannes

A landmark on Cannes' esplanade, the Martinez is a triumph of *fin-de-siècle* wedding-cake stucco architecture, with a private beach. Part of the Concorde chain of luxury hotels, it has everything you could want for a sybaritic stay. ◎ *73 blvd de la Croisette • Map G4 • 04 92 98 73 00 • martinez@concorde-hotels.com • DA • €€€€€*

3 Hôtel Noga Hilton, Cannes

Striving to out-do the longer established grand hotels of Cannes, the Noga Hilton is a relative newcomer but has out-standing modern facilities and one of the best private beaches. Like its rivals, it attracts a stellar clientele. ◎ *50 blvd de la Croisette • Map G4 • 04 92 99 70 00 • DA • €€€€*

4 Hôtel L'Aiglon, Menton

The Aiglon is set back from the crowded beach and busy traffic of the esplanade and has its own heated swimming pool, surrounded by a semi-tropical garden. It's an easy walk to the sea, but you may not want to leave this oasis. ◎ *7 rue de la Madone • Map H3 • 04 93 57 55 55 • aiglon.hotel@wanadoo.fr • €€€*

5 Le Byblos, St-Tropez

Beloved of rock stars and fashionistas, Le Byblos also has one of St-Trop's trendiest nightspots attached to it. Painted in Art Deco colours worthy of a fashion shoot (for which it is frequently used) Le Byblos is among the most luxurious hotels in Provence. ◎ *Ave Paul Signac • Map F5 • 04 94 97 00 04 • saint-tropez@byblos.com • DA • €€€€*

6 Columbus Monaco, Monaco

This new hotel aims to mix business with plea-sure – its rooms have CD players, internet access and other high-tech delights. It also has its own private beach and a fine restaurant. ◎ *23 ave des Papalins • Map H4 • 03 77 92 05 90 00 • columbus-hotel@monte-carlo.mc • DA • €€€€€*

7 Monte Carlo Beach Hotel, Roquebrune-Cap-Martin

This 46-room Art Deco showpiece has an Olympic-size pool, a cres-cent of private beach, three fine restaurants and a general air of exclusive luxury. ◎ *Ave Princesse-Grace • Map H4 • 03 77 97 97 51 00 • bh@sbm.mc • DA • €€€€*

8 Le Meridien Beach Plaza, Monte Carlo

With a private beach, two outdoor and one indoor pool, fitness centre, sauna and two restaurants and 332 rooms all with private balcony, this is one of the best hotels in Monaco. ◎ *22 ave Princesse-Grace • Map H4 • 03 77 93 30 98 80 fax 00 377 93 • www.lemeridien-montecarlo.com • DA • €€€€*

9 Hôtel la Baie Dorée, Antibes

With only 17 rooms – all but two of which have a view of the sea – this small hotel is an intimate alternative to the luxury resorts of the Riviera, with a private beach and loungers set around a tiny harbour. ◎ *579 blvd de la Garoupe • Map G4 • 04 93 67 30 67 • www.baiedoree.com • DA • €€€*

10 Résidence de la Pinede, St-Tropez

With its private beach, pool, fine sea views and excellent location, it is hardly surprising that this is a favourite with those who know St-Tropez well. ◎ *Plage de la Bouillabaisse • Map F5 • 04 94 55 91 00 • www.residencepinede.com • DA • €€€€*

Left **Oustau de la Baumanière, Les-Baux** Right **Riboto de Taven, Les-Baux**

TOP 10 Super Hideaways

1 L'Oustau de Baumanière, Les-Baux-de-Provence

This up-market boutique hotel offers exclusive luxury at a price to match. Choose from suites or rooms in a complex of beautifully restored old buildings with immaculate garden terraces and a superb restaurant. ✪ *Le Val d'Enfer • Map B4 • 04 90 54 33 07 • reception@ oustaudebaumaniere.com • DA • €€€€€*

2 Moulin de la Camandoule, Fayence

A swimming pool shaded beneath trees, excellent food, and a delightful location hidden away among vines and pines make this converted olive mill one of the most peaceful and pleasant places to stay. ✪ *Chemin de Notre-Dame-des-Cyprès • Map F4 • 04 94 76 00 84 • moulin.camandoule@ wanadoo.fr • No air conditioning • €*

3 Le Côteau Fleuri, Grimaud

High above the coast on the flanks of the Massif des Maures, this traditional inn on the outskirts of Grimaud also serves excellent food. In summer, meals are served on a pretty garden terrace with excellent views. ✪ *Pl des Pénitents • Map F5 • 04 94 43 20 17 • coteaufleuri@ wanadoo.fr • No air conditioning • €*

4 Riboto de Taven, Les-Baux-de-Provence

The "valley of hell" may seem an unlikely location for a romantic hideaway, but the Riboto de Taven, beneath the twisted rocks of the Val d'Enfer, is just that. Great scenery, gardens and a pretty pool add to its appeal. ✪ *Le Val d'Enfer • Map B4 • 04 90 53 34 23 • contact@riboto-de-taven.fr • No air conditioning • DA • €*

5 Le Cagnard, Cagnes-sur-Mer

Only a few minutes' drive from the hurly burly of the Riviera, Le Cagnard is a luxury inn, with lovely rooms in a medieval building, sweeping views and a fine restaurant. All this, and it's located in a pretty village literally drowning in bougainvillea. ✪ *Rue sous-Barri • Map G4 • 04 93 20 73 21 • www.le-cagnard.com • €€€€€*

6 Grande Bastide, St-Paul-de-Vence

This converted country house just outside St-Paul-de-Vence (too far to walk) is calm, friendly and peaceful, with a pool under palm trees and an immaculately kept garden. Rooms and suites are furnished and decorated in Provençal style, and there are pretty views. ✪ *Rte de la Colle • Map G4 • 04 93 32 50 30 • stpaulgb@lemel.fr • No air conditioning • €€€*

7 La Pérouse, Nice

A hidden luxury retreat, La Pérouse has the most outstanding views of Nice's promenade. Choose a sea-view room with its own terrace. ✪ *11 quai Rauba Capeu, • Map P5 • 04 93 62 34 63 • lp@hroy.com • €€€*

8 Hôtel les Deux Rocs, Seillans

Located in a perfectly preserved medieval hill village, Les Deux Rocs is charming in an old-fashioned way. It has a delightful terrace on a tiny cobbled square, and a good restaurant serving the best of Provençale cooking. ✪ *Pl Font d'Amont • Map F4 • 04 94 76 87 32 • No air conditioning • €*

9 La Roseraie, Vence

This friendly small hotel has a small pool and courtyard. Rooms are prettily furnished. Ideal for a romantic weekend getaway at an affordable price. ✪ *14 ave H-Giraux, rte de Cousegoules • Map G4 • 04 93 58 02 20 • No air conditioning • €*

10 La Ponche, St-Tropez

Stylish, individual and hidden away in a tiny square with a view of the fishing port, this hotel is in the perfect place to escape the mayhem of the town in summer. ✪ *3 rue des Ramparts • Map F5 • 04 94 97 02 53 • €€*

Note: Unless otherwise stated, all hotels accept credit cards, have en-suite bathrooms and air conditioning

Price Categories

For a standard, double room per night (with breakfast if included), taxes and extra charges.

€	under €100
€€	€100–€150
€€€	€150–€250
€€€€	€250–€350
€€€€€	over €350

Above **Château de la Chèvre d'Or, Eze**

🔟 Château Hotels

1 Château de la Chèvre d'Or, Eze

The wonderful Chèvre d'Or perches high above the sea, looking out over clifftop battlements in this beautifully preserved castle-village. Rooms all have a panoramic views and each one is elegantly decorated with antiques. The hotel has three fine restaurants *(see p102)* and two breathtakingly pretty pools. 🕲 *Rue du Barri • Map H4 • 04 92 10 66 66 • chevredor@relais chateaux.fr • €€€€*

2 Château de la Messardière, St-Tropez

On the outskirts of the village, this seaside palace has its own private beach and a swimming pool and is certainly among the nicest places to stay on this fashionable part of the coast. 🕲 *Rte de Tahiti • Map F5 • 04 94 56 76 00, fax 04 94 56 76 01 • www.messardiere.com/ hotel • DA • €€€€*

3 Château du Domaine St-Martin, Vence

This palatial hotel in mani-cured grounds standing on a hilltop site with views of the medieval village and the country-side is one of the most impressive places to stay in Provence. Superb ser-vice and excellent food. 🕲 *Ave des Templiers • Map G4 • 04 93 58 02 02 • st-martin@webstore.fr • DA • €€€€€*

4 Château des Alpilles, St-Rémy

Built in the 19th century, this chateau belonged to a prominent Arles family. Service standards and cuisine rate highly, and the rooms in the castle, the former chapel and adjoining converted farmhouses are very comfortable. 🕲 *Ancienne rte du Gres • Map B3 • 04 90 92 03 33 • DA • €€€*

5 Château des Ollières, Nice

This pink-and-white confection with its fairy-tale turrets and splendid, ornately painted interior, silk-covered walls and rooms full of antiques was the 19th-century home of a Russian prince. It stands within a park full of palms and deco-rative trees. 🕲 *39 ave des Baumettes • Map P4 • 04 92 15 77 99 • chateaudes ollieres@chateaudesollieres. com • No air conditioning • €€€*

6 Château de Taulane, La Martre

An hour's drive from Cannes, this magnificent 18th-century mansion has been transformed into an excellent 4-star hotel, surrounded by its own estate and an 18-hole, par 72 golf course, rated one of the best in the region. 🕲 *Le Domaine du Château de Taulane, Le Logis du Pin • Map G4 • 04 93 60 31 30 • château-de-taulane@wanadoo.fr • No air conditioning • €€€€*

7 Château de Trigance, Trigance

With just 10 rooms this small chateau, built in the 10th century and pain-stakingly restored by its owners over the last 30 years, is now a 3-star hotel with a commend-able restaurant. 🕲 *Map G4 • 04 94 76 91 18 • No air conditioning • €*

8 Château d'Allemagne, Allemagne en Provence

Listed as an historic monument, this chateau is surrounded by beauti-ful gardens. Facilities include a golf and mini-golf course *(see p114)*. 🕲 *Map E3 • 04 92 77 46 78 • himmel.doris@wanadoo.fr • DA • €€*

9 Château Eza, Eze

A wonderful collection of medieval buildings now converted into a hotel. Rooms a luxuriously decorated with Oriental rugs and marble bathrooms. 🕲 *Rue de la Pise • Map H4 • 04 93 41 12 24 • chateza@ webstore.fr • €€€€€*

10 Bastide de l'Avellane, Besse-sur-Isole

This hotel, built into the walls of a former fortified village, is surrounded by a large estate and has a pool. The restaurant serves regional dishes. 🕲 *Map E5 • 04 94 69 89 91 • avellanne@pacwan.fr • No air conditioning • €*

Left Hôtel Splendid, Cannes Right Hôtel Les Allées, Cannes

🔟 Value-for-Money Hotels

1 Hôtel Splendid, Cannes

Value for money doesn't always mean cheap, but the Splendid, centrally located close to the yacht harbour and right behind Planet Hollywood *(see p101)*, is an impressive hotel and is a bargain by Cannes standards. 🔊 *4–6 rue Felix Fauré • Map G4 • 04 93 99 53 11 • €€*

2 Le Windsor, Nice

Exotic Oriental decoration, rooms with frescoed ceilings, a pool surrounded by palm trees and, of all things, an English-style pub, come at an affordable price in this unassuming looking, medium-sized hotel. 🔊 *11 rue Dalpozzo • Map H4 • 04 93 88 59 35 • contact@ hotelwindsornice.com • €€*

3 Hôtel Les Allées, Cannes

Could this small hotel tucked away in a narrow street not far from the yacht harbour be the best bargain in Cannes? Rooms are simpe but clean and bright (some have balconies with a sea view), with phone, TV and Internet connection, and service is friendly. 🔊 *6 rue Emile-Negrin • Map G4 • 04 93 39 53 90 • info@ hotel-des-allees.com • €*

4 Le Benvengudo, Les-Baux-de-Provence

This fine hotel proves that value for money is not all about price: it has comfortable, beautifully decorated rooms (some with terraces), a pool, garden and tennis court, all in lovely surroundings near Les-Baux. 🔊 *Vallon de l'Arcoule • Map B4 • 04 90 54 32 54 • €€€*

5 Hôtel Helvetia, Monaco

This small 2-star hotel is right in the heart of Monaco, with a café-restaurant on the first floor, 25 comfortable rooms, and car parking nearby. A good budget option in an expensive destination. 🔊 *1 bis rue Grimaldi, La Condamine • Map H5 • 03 77 93 30 21 71 • hotel-helvetia@monte-carlo.mc • €*

6 Hôtel les Quatre Dauphins, Aix

This small hotel near the centre of Aix has pretty rooms on three floors, with Provençal patterned wallpaper, and modern facilities in the rooms. Service is welcoming. 🔊 *54 rue Roux Alpheran • Map C4 • 04 42 38 16 39 • No air conditioning • €*

7 Hôtel La Jabotte, Cap d'Antibes

With its clean, bright rooms and chalets and good location, La Jabotte is one of the better bargains in up-market Antibes. It also has its own car park – quite a rarity. 🔊 *13 ave Max-Maurey • Map G4 • 04 93 61 45 89 • No air conditioning • €*

8 Hôtel le Richelieu, Marseille

This very affordable hotel right on Marseille's waterfront has some rooms with balconies and lovely sea views, a nice breakfast terrace, a ground-floor terraced restaurant, and a pay beach just across the road. 🔊 *52 corniche Kennedy Ouest • Map C5 • 04 91 31 01 92 • No air conditioning • €*

9 Hôtel Européen, Marseille

One of the best places to stay in Marseille for the price, this unassuming but friendly, central, 2-star hotel has basic rooms (with washbasin and WC) as well as slightly costlier rooms with full en-suite bathroom. Sound-proofing keeps the street noise to bearable levels. 🔊 *115 rue Paradis • Map C5 • 04 91 37 77 20 • No credit cards • €*

10 Hôtel Calendal, Arles

A colourful place to stay in a colourful city, the Calendal is brightly decorated and has a very pretty, shady garden café and a comfortable tea-room. Some of the more expensive rooms have terraces and all are air conditioned, making this 2-star hotel a great-value place to stay in generally expensive Arles. 🔊 *5 rue Porte de Laure • Map B4 • 04 90 96 11 89 • €*

Note: *Unless otherwise stated, all hotels accept credit cards, have en-suite bathrooms and air conditioning*

Price Categories

For a standard, double room per night (with breakfast if included), taxes and extra charges.

€	under €100
€€	€100–€150
€€€	€150–€250
€€€€	€250–€350
€€€€€	over €350

Above **Camping International, Castellane**

🏕️10 Under Canvas Choices

1 Camping International

There are numerous camp sites in and around Castellane but this is the best of the bunch. It is close enough to shops and restaurants to be convenient, but far enough away to be untroubled by noise or traffic. The site is surrounded by fields and wooded hills, and the views are terrific. Facilities include a large swimming pool, market and a friendly, value-for-money restaurant. There are also cabins for those who do not want to stay in a tent. 🄢 *Rte Napoléon, Castellane • Map F3 • 04 92 83 66 67 • Closed Oct–Feb • No credit cards • €*

2 Camping des Oliviers

This small camp site amid olive trees on a hillside is within easy reach of Cannes and Antibes but is in a very quiet location. It has a simple snack restaurant and bar, but the main attraction is the swimming pool, on a terrace with panoramic views. 🄢 *274 Chemin des Hautes Vignasses, Biot • Map G4 • Closed Oct–Apr • No credit cards • €*

3 Camping Antipolis

The best thing about this enormous, 4-star full-service camp site is its location, just outside Antibes, minutes from the sea and with a local railway station with frequent connections into Cannes. An excellent choice for families. 🄢 *Ave du Pylone, La Brague, Antibes • Map G4 • 04 93 33 93 99 • Closed Oct–Mar • DA • €*

4 Les Cigales

Billing itself as an "open-air hotel", this very comfortable camp site just west of Cannes has spaces for tents and caravans under the olive trees, cabins and mobile homes to rent, and a large pool with a separate toddlers' lagoon. The beach is nearby, and the site is on a river with its own small quay with boats, kayaks and pedalos to rent. 🄢 *505 ave de la Mer, Mandelieu La Napoule • Map G4 • 04 93 49 23 53 • campingcigales@wanadoo.fr • €*

5 Camping la Pinède

A cheap and cheerful alternative to St Tropez's hotels – with better facilities too, including a mini-golf course, children's play area, restaurant and snack bar. 🄢 *RD 14, Grimaud • Map F5 • 04 94 56 04 36 • pinede-grimaud @wanadoo.fr • Closed mid-Oct–Mar • DA • €*

6 Camping Abri de Camargue

This clean, medium-sized camp site is near a sandy beach. The site has an indoor and outdoor pool, a children's play area, bar, shop and restaurant, and *pétanque* (boules) and tennis courts nearby. 🄢 *320 Rte du Phare de l'Espiguette, Le Grau du Roi • Map B4 • 04 66 515483 • Closed Nov–Apr • €*

7 Le Rossignol

A 3-star camp site with a pool, spaces for tents and motorhomes, and 4-person bungalows, ideal for families. 🄢 *2074 ave Jean-Michard-Pelissier, Antibes • Map G4 • 04 93 33 56 98 • Closed Oct–Mar • DA • €*

8 La Merio

This small 1-star site with space for 40 tents is in the heart of the Parc National du Mercantour *(see p40)*. Not a luxury site, but it does offer unlimited hot showers. 🄢 *1344 Rte de la Colmiane • Map G2 • 04 93 03 30 38 • Closed mid-Sep–mid-Jun • No credit cards • €*

9 Camping le Pesquier

This 2-star camp site has a small pool, and tents are pitched under shady trees. 🄢 *RN 85 Route de Digne, Castellane • Map F3 • 04 92 83 66 81 • Closed Oct–Mar • DA • €*

10 Camping les Romarins

This 2-star site is spartan, but worth it for the views along the coast. There is a snack-restaurant and bar. 🄢 *Grande Corniche, D2564, Eze • Map F3 • 04 93 01 81 64 • Closed Oct–Apr • €*

Left and right **Le Gîte de Chasteuil**

Gîte Farmhouses

1 Le Mas Dumaine
Only 2 km (1 mile) from the centre of St-Rémy, this furnished holiday home is in a traditional, stone-built farmhouse with accommodation for up to six people. There is a private swimming pool, surrounded by lawns and olive groves. ⊗ *Vieux chemin d'Arles, St-Rémy • Map B3 • 04 90 92 41 27 • No credit cards • No air conditioning • €*

2 Le Gîte de Chasteuil
This delightful bed-and-breakfast is high on a hillside in a tiny hamlet close to the east end of the Canyon du Verdon, with mountain views. For walkers, the GR4 long-distance footpath passes right through the village. Each bedroom has its own bathroom, and one has a kitchenette. ⊗ *Hameau de Chasteuil, Castellane • Map F3 • 04 92 83 72 45 • www.gitedechasteuil.com • No credit cards • No air conditioning • €*

3 Gîte d'Etape La Baume
This delightful *gîte*, nestled in a village among rocky hillsides is a great place to unwind. For swimming, the lakes of Castillon and Chaudanne are five minutes away. ⊗ *La Baume, Castellane • Map F3 • 04 92 83 70 82 • No credit cards • No en-suite bathrooms • No air conditioning • €*

4 Domaine St Joseph
Two beautifully restored farmhouses, each sleeping eight people, and a restored coach house sleeping two, stand in a private estate. Each farmhouse has its own pool, and all are filled with antique furniture, paintings and prints. Olive terraces surround the houses and the busy village of Cotignac is nearby. ⊗ *Cotignac, Var • Map D5 • 04 94 04 75 66 • eileenself@wanadoo.fr • No credit cards • DA • €*

5 La Vieille Bastide
This lovely, creeper-covered farmhouse has four bedrooms, and is set in an estate where tortoises roam and lavender, fruit trees and olives grow. It has two pools, luxury kitchen and is within walking distance of the village. ⊗ *La Garde Freinet, Golfe de St-Tropez • Map F5 • 04 94 60 00 59 • www.bastide.co.uk • No en-suite bathrooms • No air conditioning • €€€*

6 Le Moulin de Souchière
This 19th-century mill, converted into a bed-and-breakfast, stands in woodland, with streams, views of Mont Ventoux, and its own pool. There is a terrace and an open fireplace for winter. ⊗ *Entraigues-sur-la-Sorgue • Map C3 • 04 90 48 00 20 • No credit cards • No air conditioning • €*

7 Chez Bronchard
An affordable bed-and-breakfast with views of the countryside. There are three rooms, each with satellite TV and minibar, in a 200-year-old farmhouse. ⊗ *808 Chemin des Salles, La Colline de Vence, Vence • Map G4 • 04 93 24 03 66 • collin evence@libertysurf.fr • No credit cards • No air conditioning • €*

8 Le Mas de l'Esparou
This small guesthouse has views of the castle and the Alpilles mountains. The building is set in pine woods, and each of the four rooms has its own terrace. ⊗ *Rte de St-Rémy, 13520 Les-Baux-de-Provence • Map B4 • 04 90 54 41 32 • No credit cards • No air conditioning • €*

9 La Bastide Rose
This pretty farmhouse among vineyards and orchards offers three suites, a *gîte* and a private pool. ⊗ *Quartier du Gaudran, Salernes • Map B4 • 04 94 70 63 30 • labastiderose@wanadoo.fr • No credit cards • No air conditioning • €*

10 La Domaine des Coudelières
A 19th-century farmhouse, with a *gîte* and four bedrooms, decorated in Provençal style. ⊗ *560 Chemin des Coudelières, Le Thor • Map B4 • 04 90 02 12 72 • No credit cards • No air conditioning • €*

Streetsmart

Price Categories

For a standard,	€ under €100
double room per	€€ €100–€150
night (with breakfast	€€€ €150–€250
if included), taxes	€€€€ €250–€350
and extra charges.	€€€€€ over €350

Above **Hôtel de Paris**

🔟 Health and Beauty Spas

1 Hôtel Thalassothérapie

This 105-room hotel stands next to a fine sandy beach, with views of a yacht marina and the pretty port of Fréjus. It specializes in using the beneficial effects of the marine environment, including sea water, sea-weed, sand and other substances, together with the Mediterranean climate. 🟢 Port-Fréjus Ouest, Fréjus • Map F4 • DA • €€€

2 Ile Rousse Hôtel

The 4-star Ile Rousse combines the pleasures of the beach with health and beauty programmes based on its seawater spa fitness centre. The hotel has a fully-trained team and offers a range of personal programmes to bring you back to the peak of condition. 🟢 25 blvd Louis Lumière, Bandol • Map D5 • 04 94 29 33 00 • contact@ile-rousse.com • DA • €€€€

3 Hôtel Aquabella

The Romans were among the first to revere the healing properties of the thermal springs which flow from Mont Ste-Victoire, where you can take the waters in a modernized 18th-century palace, with an array of power showers, hydro-masage and mud wraps to eliminate stress and toxins. 🟢 55 cours Sextius, Aix-en-Provence • Map C4 • 04 42 23 81 81 • DA • €

4 Hôtel du Golf

Just outside Avignon, the 4-star hotel is a complex of 30 junior suites, each with whirl-pool water-therapy bath and with a range of health and beauty packages available. There are also 18- and 9-hole golf courses. 🟢 Les Chênes Verts, Vedène • Map B3 • 04 90 02 09 09 • DA • €

5 Hôtel le Méridien

On the ninth floor of one of Nice's finest luxury establishments, the hotel's beauty and fitness centre offers everything from sauna and massage to mani-cure and make-up advice. 🟢 1 Promenade des Anglais, Nice • Map G4 • 04 93 87 82 14 • DA • €€

6 Hôtel du Grand Paris

Right in the centre of the thermal resort of Digne, this luxurious hotel offers a range of treatments in the adjoining hot springs, which are used to treat arthritis, rheumatism and a range of respiratory conditions. 🟢 19 blvd Thiers, Digne-les-Bains • Map E2 • 04 92 31 11 15 • grandparis@wanadoo.fr • €€€

7 La Cremaillère

A range of spa pack-ages at the sulphur-rich thermal springs of Gréoux-les-Bains is available to guests in this farmhouse-hotel with swimming pool, golf practice range and a restaurant noted for its Provençal menu. 🟢 Rte de Riez, Greoux-les-Bains • Map E2 • 04 92 70 40 04 • www.sante-au.com • €

8 Villa Borghese

A modern hotel close to Gréoux's famous hot springs, the Borghese offers a range of menus to complement the health and beauty treatments available at the spa. Other facilities include a swimming pool, sauna and solarium. 🟢 Ave des Thermes, Gréoux-les-Bains • Map E2 • 04 92 78 00 91 • villa.borghese@wanadoo.fr • €

9 Hôtel de Paris

Monte Carlo's most glamorous hotel has direct access to the most modern health spa in Europe. The hotel also has four restaurants, its own hairdresser and luxury boutiques. 🟢 Pl du Casino, Monte Carlo • Map H3 • 03 77 92 16 49 46 • hp@sbm.mc • DA • €€€€

10 Monte Carlo Grand Hôtel

This huge hotel offers its own health spa and heated pool as well as a range of treatments offered at the nearby Thalassotherapy and Health Centre. It also has a casino, four restaurants and bar. 🟢 12 ave des Spélugues, Monte Carlo • Map H3 • 03 77 92 16 49 46 • grandhotel@monaco. mc • DA • €€€€

General Index

Acknowledgments

Main contributors
Robin Gauldie is a travel journalist who has visited Provence regularly since 1972 and divides his time between London and the South of France. After several years working for *Travel Trade Gazette*, Robin is now a freelance journalist and author of more than a dozen guidebooks to destinations ranging from Greece to Goa.

Lancashire-born Anthony Peregrine lives in the Languedoc region of southern France, and works as an author and journalist specializing in food, wine and travel. His work has appeared in the *Daily Telegraph*, *Daily Mail* and on BBC Radio 4.

Produced by Sargasso Media Ltd, London

Project Editor Zoë Ross
Designer Stephen Woosnam-Savage
Picture Research Monica Allende
Proofreader Stewart J Wild
Editorial Assistance Sophie Warne

Main Photographer Demetrio Carrasco

Additional Photography Max Alexander, Robin Gauldie, John Heseltine, Kim Sayer, Alan Williams

Illustrator Chris Orr & Associates

FOR DORLING KINDERSLEY
Senior Art Editor Marisa Renzullo
Senior Publishing Manager Louise Lang
Publishing Managers Kate Poole, Helen Townsend
Art Director Gillian Allan
Cartography Co-ordinator Casper Morris
DTP Jason Little
Production Joanna Bull, Marie Ingledew

Maps James Anderson

Special Assistance
The authors would like to thank Ann Noon, Maison de la France, London; Sybil Darrington, Monaco Visitor and Convention Bureau; Sandra Jurinic, Office de Tourisme et des Congrès, Nice; Yvonne Perettoni, Office de Tourisme, Marseille; Danielle Damiani, Comité Départemental de Tourisme, Vaucluse; Hoverspeed

Picture Credits
t-top; tc-top centre; tr-top right; cla-centre left above; ca-centre above; cra-centre right above; cl-centre left; c-centre; cr-centre right; clb-centre left below; cb-centre below; crb-centre right below; bl-below left; bc-below centre; br-below right.

Acknowledgments

The publishers would like to thank the following individuals, companies, and picture libraries for permission to reproduce their photographs:

© Succession Picasso/DACS 2002 "Ceramic Jug" Picasso 93t, © ADAGP,Paris and DACS, London 2002 Chagall 105t

AISA, Barcelona: 7tr, 7c, 12b, 20-21c, 24-25c; AKG, London: 34tr, 37r, © ADAGP, Paris/ DACS, London 2002 "Manteau de porte" Maillol 34b, © ADAGP, Paris/Dacs, London 2002 "*Sailing boats in the harbour of St Tropez*" Paul Signac 35r, © ADAGP, Paris and DACS, London 2002 "*Jetée d'Honfleur*" Raoul Dufy 36tl, © Succession Picasso/ DACS 2002 "*Self-Portrait*" Picasso 36tr, "*La Montagne Sainte-Victoire, vue de Bibemus*" Cézanne 36b, "*Lilac Bush*", Vincent van Gogh 37t, Cameraphoto Epoche 29t, Erich Lessing 29r, Lothar Peter 35t

CEPHAS: Mick Rock 52tl, 52tr, 52b, 53r; CORBIS: 6cl, 56b, 57r, 58t, 58b, 59c, 59r, 80-81

Jacket: All special photography except Corbis: Paul Almasy B/C top centre; Ric Ergenbright B/C top right; Owen Franken F/C main image and bottom; Nik Wheeler B/C top left.

All other images are ©DK for further information see www.dkimages.com

Dorling Kindersley Special Editions

Dorling Kindersley books can be purchased in bulk quantities at discounted prices for use in promotions or as premiums. We are also able to offer special editions and personalized jackets, corporate imprints, and excerpts from all of our books, tailored specifically to meet your own needs.

To find out more, please contact: (in the United Kingdom) – Special Sales, Dorling Kindersley Limited, 80 Strand, London WC2R ORL; (in the United States) – Special Markets Department, Dorling Kindersley, Inc., 375 Hudson Street, New York, NY 10014.

Phrase Book

In Emergency

Help!	**Au secours!**	oh sekoor
Stop!	**Arrêtez!**	aret-ay
Call a doctor!	**Appelez un médecin!**	apuh-lay uñ medsañ
Call an ambulance!	**Appelez une ambulance!**	apuh-lay oon oñboo-loñs
Call the police!	**Appelez la police!**	apuh-lay lah poh-lees
Call the fire brigade!	**Appelez les pompiers!**	apuh-lay leh poñ-peeyay

Communication Essentials

Yes/No	**Oui/Non**	wee/noñ
Please	**S'il vous plaît**	seel voo play
Thank you	**Merci**	mer-see
Excuse me	**Excusez-moi**	exkoo-zay mwah
Hello	**Bonjour**	boñzhoor
Goodbye	**Au revoir**	oh ruh-vwar
Good night	**Bonsoir**	boñ-swar
What?	**Quel, quelle?**	kel, kel
When?	**Quand?**	koñ
Why?	**Pourquoi?**	poor-kwah
Where?	**Où?**	oo

Useful Phrases

How are you?	**Comment allez-vous?**	kom-moñ talay voo
Very well, thank you.	**Très bien,**	treh byañ
Pleased to meet you.	**Enchanté de faire votre connaissance.**	oñshoñ-tay duh fehr votr kon-ay sans
Where is/are...?	**Où est/sont...?**	oo ay/soñ
Which way to...?	**Quelle est la direction pour...?**	kel ay lah deer-ek-syoñ poor
Do you speak English?	**Parlez-vous anglais?**	par-lay voo oñg-lay
I don't understand.	**Je ne comprends pas.**	zhuh nuh kom-proñ pah
I'm sorry.	**Excusez-moi.**	exkoo-zay mwah

Useful Words

big	**grand**	groñ
small	**petit**	puh-tee
hot	**chaud**	show
cold	**froid**	frwah
good	**bon**	boñ
bad	**mauvais**	moh-veh
open	**ouvert**	oo-ver
closed	**fermé**	fer-meh
left	**gauche**	gohsh
right	**droit**	drwah
entrance	**l'entrée**	l'on-tray
exit	**la sortie**	sor-tee

Shopping

How much does this cost?	**C'est combien s'il vous plaît?**	say kom-byañ seel voo play
I would like ...	**je voudrais...**	zhuh voo-dray
Do you have?	**Est-ce que vous avez?**	es-kuh voo zavay
Do you take credit cards?	**Est-ce que vous acceptez les cartes de crédit?**	es-kuh voo zaksept-ay leh kart duh kreh-dee
What time do you open?	**A quelle heure vous êtes ouvert?**	ah kel urr voo zet oo-ver
What time do you close?	**A quelle heure vous êtes fermé?**	ah kel urr voo zet fer-may
This one.	**Celui-ci.**	suhl-wee-see
That one.	**Celui-là.**	suhl-wee-lah
expensive	**cher**	shehr
cheap	**pas cher, bon marché**	pah shehr, boñ mar-shay
size, clothes	**la taille**	tye
size, shoes	**la pointure**	pwañ-tur
white	**blanc**	bloñ
black	**noir**	nwahr
red	**rouge**	roozh
yellow	**jaune**	zhohwn
green	**vert**	vehr
blue	**bleu**	blur

Types of Shop

antique shop	**le magasin d'antiquités**	maga-zañ d'oñteekee-tay
bakery	**la boulangerie**	booloñ-zhuree
bank	**la banque**	boñk
bookshop	**la librairie**	lee-brehree
cake shop	**la pâtisserie**	patee-sree
cheese shop	**la fromagerie**	fromazh-ree
chemist	**la pharmacie**	farmah-see
department store	**le grand magasin**	groñ maga-zañ
delicatessen	**la charcuterie**	sharkoot-ree
gift shop	**le magasin de cadeaux**	maga-zañ duh kadoh
greengrocer	**le marchand de légumes**	mar-shoñ duh lay-goom
grocery	**l'alimentation**	alee-moñta-syoñ
market	**le marché**	marsh-ay
newsagent	**le magasin de journaux**	maga-zañ duh zhoor-no
post office	**la poste, le bureau de poste, le PTT**	pohst, booroh duh pohst, peh-teh-teh
supermarket	**le supermarché**	soo pehr-marshay
tobacconist	**le tabac**	tabah
travel agent	**l'agence de voyages**	l'azhoñs duh vwayazh

Sightseeing

abbey	**l'abbaye**	l'abay-ee
art gallery	**la galerie d'art**	galer-ree dart
bus station	**la gare routière**	gahr roo-tee-yehr
cathedral	**la cathédrale**	katay-dral
church	**l'église**	l'aygleez
garden	**le jardin**	zhar-dañ
library	**la bibliothèque**	beeblee-o-tek
museum	**le musée**	moo-zay
railway station	**la gare (SNCF)**	gahr (es-en-say-ef)
tourist information office	**renseignements touristiques, le syndicat d'initiative**	roñsayn-moñ toorees-teek, sandee-ka d'eenee-syateev
town hall	**l'hôtel de ville**	l'ohtel duh veel

Staying in a Hotel

Do you have a vacant room?	**Est-ce que vous avez une chambre?**	essкuh voo zavay oon shambr

double room, with double bed	**la chambre à deux personnes, avec un grand lit**	shambr ah duh pehr-son avek un gronñ lee
twin room	**la chambre à deux lits**	shambr ah duh lee
single room	**la chambre à une personne**	shambr ah oon pehr-son
room with a bath, shower	**la chambre avec salle de bains, une douche**	shambr avek sal duh bañ, oon doosh
I have a reservation.	**J'ai fait une réservation.**	zhay fay oon rayzehrva-syoñ

Eating Out

Have you got a table?	**Avez-vous une table de libre?**	avay-voo oon tahbl duh leebr
I want to reserve a table.	**Je voudrais réserver une table.**	zhuh voo-dray rayzehr-vay oon tahbl
The bill please.	**L'addition s'il vous plaît.**	l'adee-syoñ seel voo play
Waitress/ waiter	**Madame, Mademoiselle/ Monsieur**	mah-dam, mah-demwahzel/ muh-syuh
menu	**le menu, la carte**	men-oo, kart
fixed-price menu	**le menu à prix fixe**	men-oo ah pree feeks
cover charge	**le couvert**	koo-vehr
wine list	**la carte des vins**	kart-deh vañ
glass	**le verre**	vehr
bottle	**la bouteille**	boo-tay
knife	**le couteau**	koo-toh
fork	**la fourchette**	for-shet
spoon	**la cuillère**	kwee-yehr
breakfast	**le petit déjeuner**	puh-tee deh-zhuh-nay
lunch	**le déjeuner**	deh-zhuh-nay
dinner	**le dîner**	dee-nay
main course	**le plat principal**	plah prañsee-pal
starter, first course	**l'entrée, le hors d'oeuvre**	l'oñ-tray, or-duhvr
dish of the day	**le plat du jour**	plah doo zhoor
wine bar	**le bar à vin**	bar ah vañ
café	**le café**	ka-fay

Menu Decoder

baked	**cuit au four**	kweet oh foor
beef	**le boeuf**	buhf
beer	**la bière**	bee-yehr
boiled	**bouilli**	boo-yee
bread	**le pain**	pan
butter	**le beurre**	burr
cake	**le gâteau**	gah-toh
cheese	**le fromage**	from-azh
chicken	**le poulet**	poo-lay
chips	**les frites**	freet
chocolate	**le chocolat**	shoko-lah
coffee	**le café**	kah-fay
dessert	**le dessert**	deh-ser
egg	**l'oeuf**	l'uf
fish	**le poisson**	pwah-ssoñ
fresh fruit	**le fruit frais**	frwee freh
garlic	**l'ail**	l'eye
grilled	**grillé**	gree-yay
ham	**le jambon**	zhoñ-boñ
ice, ice cream	**la glace**	glas
lamb	**l'agneau**	l'anyoh
lemon	**le citron**	see-troñ
meat	**la viande**	vee-yand

milk	**le lait**	leh
mineral water	**l'eau minérale**	l'oh meeney-ral
oil	**l'huile**	l'weel
onions	**les oignons**	leh zonyoñ
fresh orange juice	**l'orange pressée**	l'oroñzh press-eh
fresh lemon juice	**le citron pressé**	see-troñ press-eh
pepper	**le poivre**	pwavr
pork	**le porc**	por
potatoes	**pommes de terre**	pom-duh tehr
rice	**le riz**	ree
roast	**rôti**	row-tee
salt	**le sel**	sel
sausage, fresh	**la saucisse**	sohsees
seafood	**les fruits de mer**	frwee duh mer
snails	**les escargots**	leh zes-kar-goh
soup	**la soupe, le potage**	soop, poh-tazh
steak	**le bifteck**	beef-tek, stek
sugar	**le sucre**	sookr
tea	**le thé**	tay
vegetables	**les légumes**	lay-goom
vinegar	**le vinaigre**	veenaygr
water	**l'eau**	l'oh
red wine	**le vin rouge**	vañ roozh
white wine	**le vin blanc**	vañ bloñ

Numbers

0	**zéro**	zeh-roh
1	**un, une**	uñ, oon
2	**deux**	duh
3	**trois**	trwah
4	**quatre**	katr
5	**cinq**	sañk
6	**six**	sees
7	**sept**	set
8	**huit**	weet
9	**neuf**	nerf
10	**dix**	dees
11	**onze**	oñz
12	**douze**	dooz
13	**treize**	trehz
14	**quatorze**	katorz
15	**quinze**	kañz
16	**seize**	sehz
17	**dix-sept**	dees-set
18	**dix-huit**	dees-weet
19	**dix-neuf**	dees-nerf
20	**vingt**	vañ
30	**trente**	tront
40	**quarante**	karoñt
50	**cinquante**	sañkoñt
60	**soixante**	swasoñt
70	**soixante-dix**	swasoñt-dees
80	**quatre-vingts**	katr-vañ
90	**quatre-vingt-dix**	katr-vañ-dees
100	**cent**	soñ
1,000	**mille**	meel

Time

one minute	**une minute**	oon mee-noot
one hour	**une heure**	oon urr
half an hour	**une demi-heure**	urr duh-me urr
one day	**un jour**	urr zhorr
Monday	**lundi**	luñ-dee
Tuesday	**mardi**	mar-dee
Wednesday	**mercredi**	mehrkruh-dee
Thursday	**jeudi**	zhuh-dee
Friday	**vendredi**	voñdruh-dee
Saturday	**samedi**	sam-dee
Sunday	**dimanche**	dee-moñsh